Together We Learn

Judy Clarke

Ron Wideman

Susan Eadie

Prentice-Hall Canada Inc., Scarborough, Ontario

Canadian Cataloguing in Publication Data

Clarke, Judy
   Together we learn

Includes bibliographical references.
ISBN 0-13-924556-1

1. Group work in education.   2. Team learning
approach in education. I. Wideman, Ron.
II. Eadie, Susan J. (Susan Jane),   . date
III. Title.

LB1032.C58 1990   371.3'95   C90-093019-5

PRENTICE-HALL, INC., Englewood Cliffs, New Jersey
PRENTICE-HALL INTERNATIONAL INC., London
PRENTICE-HALL OF AUSTRALIA, PTY., LTD., Sydney
PRENTICE-HALL OF INDIA, PVT., LTD., New Delhi
PRENTICE-HALL OF JAPAN, INC., Tokyo
PRENTICE-HALL OF SOUTHEAST ASIA (PTE.) LTD., Singapore
EDITORA PRENTICE-HALL DO BRASIL, LTDA., Rio de Janeiro
PRENTICE-HALL HISPANOAMERICANA, S.A., Mexico

ISBN 0-13-924556-1

Production Editor: Jessica Pegis
Manufacturing Buyer: Crystale Chalmers
Design: Lorne Moore
Cover: Gail Ferreira-Ng-A-Kien
Typesetting and Graphics: Tony Gordon Ltd.

   3 4 5 6 AP 95 94 93 92

Printed and bound in Canada by The Alger Press Limited.

Preface

Together We Learn is the product of a successful collaborative group effort.

The original edition was prepared co-operatively by and for The Board of Education for the Borough of East York, The Board of Education for the City of Etobicoke, The Board of Education for the City of North York, The Board of Education for the City of Scarborough, The Board of Education for the City of Toronto and The Board of Education for the City of York, under the auspices of The Metropolitan Toronto School Board.

In 1987 a proposal to develop *Together We Learn* was endorsed by a committee of superintendents of curriculum of The Metropolitan Toronto School Board. The writers worked with an advisory group from the six boards as well as reviewers and fieldtesters to develop the document. It was completed and published by The Metropolitan Toronto School Board in 1988.

In 1989 The Metropolitan Toronto School Board contracted with Prentice-Hall Canada to publish this national edition of *Together We Learn*. One of the major differences between the original and national editions is that the national one has expanded the focus from co-operative learning in grades 7, 8, 9 and 10 to all grade levels, from primary to adult education. The current edition is designed as a useful tool for teachers in all subject areas and at all grade levels across the country.

Additionally, the chapter on evaluation has been extended from the original edition to provide more information and evaluation forms and worksheets suitable for students of all ages.

Together We Learn has been designed as a practical "how-to" handbook to help teachers implement small group learning strategies in their classrooms. The book offers the following to teachers:

- A practical nuts-and-bolts approach to co-operative learning that provides a student classroom suggestions and aids.
- Thorough coverage of co-operative learning approaches to assist teachers of varying levels of experience with group work.
- Suggestions that are relevant to all grades, disciplines and students.
- A jargon-free easy-to-read treatment of co-operative learning techniques.

The writing team wishes to acknowledge Mark Brubacher for his most helpful contributions during the early development stages of the project. The advisory board members — Elizabeth Coelho, Craig Crone, Wayne Fairhead, Jane Gibson and Suzanne Ziegler — are much appreciated for their participation throughout, for the initial guidance they provided, for the large number of field testers and reviewers they organized, and for their unwavering support and critical response through the challenging and exciting evolution of *Together We Learn*.

Judy Clarke
Ron Wideman
Susan Eadie

Table of Contents

1 Introduction

While working in small groups I can voice my own opinions and have everybody listen to me and consider my thoughts. I can also take criticism more easily because, since it is a small group, people take into consideration what you say and what you are trying to say. You see, I am a shy person. It may not seem that way in class, but I am. For the shy person it is a boost of the ego to be in a small group. Everyone encourages one another and helps the other person to have courage.

Mary, Grade 10

In co-operative learning my students become more responsible because they have a sense of ownership for their work and get encouragement from peers. They come to class on time and they get to work more quickly. They are aware that they are responsible to themselves and to their friends, not just to me. I'm getting comments from employers that students in my business courses are getting along well with others and that they are responsible.

Secondary Teacher of Business Studies

Sometimes students think teachers know everything. In small group learning students seek help and ideas from each other. Sometimes they have wonderful ideas that you couldn't have thought of as the teacher.

Elementary Teacher

The self-confidence students develop in small group learning carries over to participation in larger groups. I've had students come to tell me that they are not afraid now to contribute in debates and discussions in other classes.

Secondary Teacher

Introduction

Co-operative small group learning is an approach to organizing classroom activity so that students can interact with and learn from one another as well as from the teacher and the world around them. Whether they are working in pairs, or groups of three or four or five, students in a co-operative setting build on one another's ideas and strengths to learn more effectively.

For example, a teacher of grade nine general level mathematics noticed that students were having difficulty following instructions to solve mathematics problems. She found an activity in which students had to follow instructions to construct a pentagon by folding and making one cut in a piece of paper.

Many teachers might have asked students to complete the activity individually without talking. This teacher asked students to form groups of three to work on the problem. Each group was to follow the instructions to build one pentagon.

The teacher remembers how successful the activity was. All students were actively engaged throughout the period. All groups were able to complete the task. Students were successful because the group context required them to think through the instructions by talking them through together.

At one table, three students were leaning forward intently, "putting their heads together." The group had folded the piece of paper in half, left over right, according to step two in the instructions. Michael was labelling the corners of the folded page, F, A, E, D. The group was puzzling out step three.

Nayoung said, "It looks like the dotted lines on the diagrams show where the paper should be folded."

"Ah!" said Kelly, "Then we have to mark the paper halfway between F and A to know where to make the next fold."

"Where is the ruler?" asked Michael. "And we'd better check step four to make sure we're okay before going on." The group paused to discuss how to proceed.

In the activity, academic, personal, and social goals of education were pursued simultaneously. Students learned about the properties of pentagons and about following instructions. The academic learning process was furthered by the opportunity to exchange and test ideas. The experience that each member had of contributing usefully to the effort built feelings of self-assurance and competence. Students listened to each other and helped each other understand.

Successful small group learning activities such as these don't happen automatically. These students had been working in groups for some time. The teacher had set the stage by cultivating a classroom climate of respect and care. She had systematically observed previous group activities, and she had taught needed group skills. She was happy to see academic learning increase as group interaction improved.

Co-operative learning methods are effective with students of all ages, from kindergarten level through continuing (adult) education. Since most examples can also be adapted for use in other contexts, the handbook is truly a resource for all teachers.

Three Reasons to Use Co-operative Small Group Learning

Co-operative small group learning is a tried and proven approach for organizing classroom activity. While there are many reasons to recommend it to teachers, three reasons are important to emphasize at the outset.

Effective Schools

Co-operative small group learning promotes effective schools which contribute to the academic, personal and social development of students.

There is a large body of research which demonstrates how co-operative learning contributes to improved student outcomes. Co-operative learning produces higher academic achievement, more effective problem solving, increased use of higher-level thinking skills, more positive attitudes toward subject matter, and greater motivation to learn.

Research also indicates that co-operative small group learning fosters stronger feelings of self-worth. Students feel accepted by peers and more able to learn. Students assume greater responsibility for their actions and develop co-operative skills. They learn values such as respect and caring for others, responsibility, helpfulness, and empathy.

Effective schools must be concerned with the both the cognitive and affective development of students. Through co-operative learning, teachers can provide a strong academic program and, at the same time, attend to the personal and social development objectives of education.

Race and Ethnic Relations

Co-operative small group learning capitalizes on the diverse population of the public schools to promote positive race and ethnic relations.

The rich diversity of the population of the public schools provides unique opportunities for people of many different backgrounds to develop a lifelong appreciation of others. The research evidence demonstrates that in schools of diverse population, co-operative small group learning builds respect for others regardless of race, creed, colour, sex, or background. Reviewing the research, Robert Slavin in his article "Cooperative Learning" (*Review of Education Research,* Summer 1980) concludes that fostering interracial co-operation is by far the most effective means of improving racial attitudes and behaviours in schools.

By assigning students of different backgrounds to work together, the teacher is telling students that he/she approves of and expects interracial interaction and co-operation. This is a powerful position — more pro-active than simply taking a stand against racial name-calling and other negative behaviours.

Working in co-operative small groups <u>integrates everyone by placing students on an equal basis with equal responsibilities</u>. As students work together they share common goals and challenges. As small groups change within classrooms, students work with and get to know many other classmates. It is this integrated co-operative environment which breaks down stereotypes and fosters appreciation of people as individuals with unique talents regardless of origin or heritage.

Equity in Education

Co-operative small group learning maximizes equality of educational opportunity.

Research evidence demonstrates that <u>all students benefit</u> from the equality of educational opportunity provided in the co-operative small group setting. Students are active partners in learning with responsibilities for themselves and their classmates. The learning environment which results promotes positive self-image and improved learning, particularly for students who might otherwise be at risk. This includes male students in primary classes, female students in mathematics and science classes, and learning disabled students integrated in regular classes.

Research often identifies lack of facility with standard Canadian English as a major reason for lower academic achievement. Traditional teacher-centred instruction restricts the use of language by having students sit individually and not talk with others. Learning without talking through ideas and information is difficult for most people. Students whose language or culture differ from the majority suffer the greatest disadvantage. In contrast to teacher-centred instruction, co-operative small group interaction provides the intense engagement in communication and peer collegiality which equalizes access to learning. The discussion process in small groups helps students to ask questions and negotiate meaning as they use language.

Benefits for Students

A solid body of research, including over 800 studies conducted over 25 years, establishes that co-operative small group learning benefits students in the following ways.

① Academic Learning

Students' academic achievement improves. Low-achieving and average students show the greatest gains.

Students develop more positive attitudes toward the subject matter and a greater motivation to learn.

Students learn more effective problem-solving skills and the use of higher-level thinking skills.

Students explore ideas at appropriate levels of thinking, through watching, experimenting, and talking with peers.

Students feel free to develop their own understandings and are less concerned about adopting the teacher's viewpoint as the only one.

Students develop communication skills as they talk and learn with peers. This regular opportunity for discussion is particularly important given the large number of students in Canadian schools for whom English is a second language.

Student language is more elaborate in extended peer exchanges than in student-teacher short answer interchange. More elaborate language is accompanied by more elaborate and advanced thinking.

Working with peers helps students relate curriculum content to their own interests, life experiences and values. This is essential for meaningful learning to occur.

Working in groups teaches students to develop responsibility for their own learning and the learning of others.

✦ ② Personal and Social Development

Students develop more positive self-image. They feel accepted by peers and more able to learn.

Students learn about themselves from interacting with others. They become aware of their own strengths and difficulties. They develop a sense of being valued team members and learn how to function in a group more effectively.

Students become actively involved in taking responsibility for themselves and their learning.

Students learn and practise co-operative skills. They feel more in command of their own participation and better able to influence and support others in positive directions.

Students develop positive attitudes toward others. As they develop co-operative skills, they learn values such as respect and caring for others, responsibility, helpfulness and empathy.

Students learn about peers from interacting with them rather than from watching classmates interacting with the teacher. Working together helps students to break down stereotypes and to understand the many dimensions and abilities of others.

Benefits for Teachers

It is not only students who benefit from co-operative small group learning. Teachers also benefit in the following ways.

① Achieving Balanced Curriculum Objectives

Co-operative small group learning provides ways for students to learn values and practise collaborative skills within the context of regular classroom work, whether that be in mathematics, auto mechanics, visual arts, or in a second language. Co-operative small group learning enables the teacher to provide a balanced curriculum which simultaneously addresses academic, personal, and social development objectives, including:

- promoting active learning;
- promoting academic competence;
- improving self-esteem;
- developing respect for others;
- improving race relations;
- facilitating language across the curriculum;
- integrating students with special needs;
- managing bi-level and multi-level classes;
- responding to a variety of learning styles.

② More Positive Student Attitudes

Teachers appreciate the enthusiasm and energy for learning which co-operative small group activity generates among students. Specifically, students exhibit:

- peer sanction and support for the academic effort of all members in the class;
- more positive attitudes toward subject matter and increased liking for the teacher and school;
- increased positive relationships with peers.

③ A Wider Variety of Interesting Roles

Co-operative small group learning frees the teacher to assume a wider variety of roles in the classroom. Teachers spend more time as facilitators, observers and participants. They spend less time as dispensers of information and supervisors of students' behaviour.

Teachers find they have greater flexibility and increased opportunity for creativity in approaching existing curricula.

Teachers have increased time and opportunity to observe students actively involved in learning.

Teachers have greater opportunities to get to know students and observe dimensions of student behaviour and needs that would not be apparent during teacher-directed instruction. Information gained through observation is requisite to planning a program appropriate to students' abilities and needs.

How Co-operative Small Group Learning Works

Co-operative small group learning is based on five common principles. Teachers whose group work is successful will generally find that they are applying these principles intuitively. Using the five principles intentionally to structure classroom activity enables teachers to improve the effectiveness of their small group activities. The five principles are:

1. Students work in positive interdependence;
2. Students work in small heterogeneous groups;
3. Students are accountable both as individuals and as a group;
4. Students learn through ample opportunity for purposeful talk;
5. Students learn and practise co-operative skills as they study and explore the subject matter together.

Principle #1

Students work in positive interdependence.

Co-operative small group activities are structured so that students work together in ways to support one another's learning. Co-operative learning provides opportunities for all students to develop and to believe in their ability to contribute and to learn from others. Positive interdependence among students in a class helps to build a supportive and cohesive environment. It provides the foundation for co-operative small group learning to flourish.

One weakness of traditional approaches to group work has been that groups were often given tasks which could just as easily have been done by individuals working alone. In contrast, to succeed in a co-operative small group learning task, students are engaged actively in working together.

how do I do it

In general, positive interdependence is achieved by setting and working toward common goals while at the same time assigning appropriate individual work responsibilities.

Principle #2

Students work in small heterogeneous groups.

Groups are usually small to encourage interaction and verbal interchange among students. Though pairs can often be used, groups of four or five are optimal for most discussions and tasks. Beyond this size it is hard for groups to function without a formal leader.

Heterogeneous grouping based on ethnicity, gender, ability, and personality brings various talents and ways of thinking to bear on problems. Heterogeneity mirrors the real world of encountering, accepting, and appreciating differences. The diverse population of the public schools provides unique opportunities to combat racism and foster appreciation for one another. But to do this, students must have an opportunity to interact frequently and on personal terms. Heterogeneous groupings provide such opportunities as students work together co-operatively on common tasks.

Same-ability groupings are generally considered to have a negative impact on the class as a whole. However, teachers should feel free to use interest and random groupings as well as carefully selected heterogeneous groupings depending on the nature of the activities and the personality of the class.

Principle #3

Students are accountable both as individuals and as a group.

The purpose of small group work is to maximize the learning of each student. Individuals must clearly understand their responsibilities within the group and in relation to other groups. In co-operative small group learning, the group interaction and the task are organized so that individual student effort is valued by others. Students develop initiative and responsibility for their own learning and the learning of other members in their group. A balance of individual and group accountability is, therefore, a natural outcome of the co-operative process.

Principle #4

Students learn through ample opportunity for purposeful talk.

Dialogue is at the heart of learning. In order to assimilate new experience and integrate it with their own, students need to think through ideas. The best way for most people to think through ideas is to talk them through. Talk is the way people explore ideas, clarify them, and personalize information and experience.

When students collaborate, either to learn new information or to accomplish a task, they need time to be tentative before coming to more definite conclusions. Students need to be reassured that talk is an important vehicle for understanding.

Principle #5

Students learn and practise co-operative skills as they study and explore the subject matter together.

Working collaboratively requires the use of co-operative skills. Many traditional approaches to group work do not teach these skills. Co-operative small group learning methods do. The process involves working together, reflecting on the experience, understanding something about working together, and practising that learning in subsequent rounds of group activity.

The need for student reflection on both process and product cannot be overemphasized. Whether it is done through explicit instruction or informal discussion, the teacher's role is to ensure that students learn the co-operative skills needed to work effectively together.

One Teacher's Experience

A grade eight Family Studies teacher made role-taking activities more involving, more effective and less threatening by using a variation of the co-operative small group learning method called Jigsaw. The activity he designed illustrates the use of the five principles on which co-operative small group learning is based. For more information on Jigsaw see Chapters Three and Four.

The class of twenty students was exploring a case study involving family relationships. The teacher organized the class into five home groups of four students each. Male and female students of various abilities and backgrounds were placed in each home group. Each student in each group was assigned a different role to play — mother, father, sister, brother — and given a page which described the case study situation and defined the problem to be solved. Each home group talked briefly about the situation and the problem without going into role.

Then the teacher reorganized the class into four exploration groups of five students each. All the fathers met in one exploration group, all the mothers in another, all the sisters in another, and all the brothers in another. In these groups students were given an information sheet about the character they were playing. Each group talked about how the particular character they were assigned might act in the situation and how they might want the problem solved. They speculated on how the other characters would act and what they would want. Together they rehearsed how they would play the role.

Then students returned to their home groups. In these groups they played their respective roles as the family in question tried to solve the problem it was having. Students participated enthusiastically in the spirited dialogue. Then each home group talked about how the family it portrayed had operated, why various members acted as they did, and how the behaviour of members affected the behaviour of other members.

Later, students returned to their exploration groups to further debrief the role play. For example, the mothers talked about their experiences during the role play and speculated about what might have happened differently if they or others had acted differently. They talked about what they had learned about the problems families have.

At the conclusion of the activity, each student handed in a short paper describing what he or she had learned about family interactions. In addition, exploration groups filled out evaluation sheets assessing how effectively they had functioned. Because time management was identified by a number of groups as a problem, the teacher presented some tips on how to organize time. In subsequent group work sessions students were asked to pay particular attention to improving time management using the tips which they had learned.

The activity described above was effective because the teacher had incorporated all of the five principles on which co-operative small group learning is based. Students worked in positive interdependence. Each student had a contribution to make because each had a role to play. The information sheets about the characters gave each student information about the situation that other students in different roles did not have. Students in the exploration groups helped each other understand the roles and plan their participation.

Students worked in small heterogeneous groups. Everyone could participate in the role play, not just a few at one time. The heterogeneity of each group enriched learning by bringing a wide variety of backgrounds to the discussion in each group.

Students were accountable both as individuals and as groups. In the home groups, students were accountable for their roles. The exploration groups were accountable for preparing their members. At the conclusion of the activity each student handed in a paper for evaluation by the teacher and each exploration group was evaluated by its members for effectiveness.

Students had ample opportunity to talk. Discussion was integral to the entire process. In addition, the small group approach to role playing allowed each student to participate actively and to reflect on his/her experience with others who had had the same experience.

Students learned a co-operative skill which they identified from their experience as important to group effectiveness. The teacher built in opportunity to reflect on group process and actively taught the needed skill. Students had opportunities to practise that skill in later group work sessions.

Summary

In this chapter we have described the five underlying principles which set co-operative small group learning apart from traditional group work. We have identified the reasons why educators are excited by the potential of co-operative small group learning. Students share this enthusiasm. In the words of one student:

Working with a small group I found to be interesting for a number of reasons. For once you feel independent. For the first time you are not the sponge to sit and listen to someone lecturing. You, yourself, are the teacher and so are all the members in your group. Everyone explains the ideas, so all the members can learn from each other.

For the first time you have a choice whether to learn and understand a new concept. You have the choice to grasp and deeply explore the subject. You could go beyond the topic and your horizons and really learn something. I also found that once someone said something you could go beyond that idea. One idea brings you to many others.

One last thing I've learned is that people are not threatened to speak, whereas when you're in a class of 30 or more students you are somewhat withholding of questions for reasons of embarrassment. People in my group who are really quiet in class felt compelled to speak and contribute to the talk. It was so much easier talking and opening up to new ideas.

In conclusion, I just would like to give my views on co-operative group activity. If this is what education has in store for the children of the next generation, school will have so much more to offer children other than a credit. School could be a great learning experience like it should be. I really hope university reviews its way of teaching and opens the doors to group activity for success would be much greater.

Angelo, Grade 12

2 Starting Group Work

Being in a group and studying opens up your mind to many different interpretations of one idea. I know it opened my mind. In the group I also learned about different people and their views.

Aly, Grade 8

Successful co-operative learning activities are dependent upon an interplay of these five principles.

1. Students work in positive interdependence.

2. Students work in small heterogeneous groups.

3. Students are accountable both as individuals and as a group.

4. Students learn through ample opportunity for purposeful talk.

5. Students learn and practise co-operative skills as they study and explore the subject matter together.

These principles are introduced in Chapter One and included as part of discussion in Chapter Two. Chapters Three and Four demonstrate how the principles work in practical application. Chapters Five and Six provide information on the teaching of co-operative skills. Chapter Seven describes evaluation methods.

About three weeks after I started using co-operative learning I noticed a friendly feeling in the classroom. The students enjoy and are supportive of each other. They listen carefully to each other, ask questions and help each other. Small group work has made it possible for me to move around and to get to know the students from watching them work together.

Secondary Teacher

Co-operative learning takes practice — for the teacher as well as for the students. With experience, I'm learning to spot social skills the students need to learn during their group work.

Several Secondary and Elementary Teachers

Co-operative learning is a wonderful opportunity for the students who tend to be shy to become involved, and it's nice to see the other students appreciate their contributions.

Elementary Teacher

Starting Group Work

Learning to work productively in small groups is a gradual and developmental process which requires careful planning on the part of the teacher. There are many ways teachers help students learn to work successfully in groups.

This chapter offers suggestions for teachers planning to introduce small group work to their students. These suggestions are organized into five general categories:

- Providing Rationale and Reassurance;
- Observing Students to Generate New Understandings;
- Building in Reflection Right from the Start;
- Designing Beginning Group Activities;
- Informing Parents.

The suggestions offered are neither a prescriptive list, nor an exhaustive one. Rather, they represent some ways that teachers start group work with their students.

Teachers experienced in using small groups may find these suggestions familiar, and helpful in enriching current directions in their work. These teachers may wish to browse through this chapter, experiment with a few ideas, and then move on to the next six chapters for further professional development.

Teachers who have not had experience in using small groups will find that the suggestions in this chapter provide a practical guide for beginning their group work. These teachers can experiment with the ideas and examples at a pace appropriate to the development of both themselves and their classes.

Providing Rationale and Reassurance

Often teachers introduce group work by telling students what they are going to be doing and why, for example, sharing with students the rationale provided in Chapter One. Students need to understand the teacher's commitment to group work to begin to develop positive attitudes toward working in groups.

As well, teachers can provide reassurance that learning to work in groups is a gradual process which will require the practice, patience, and support of all class members. It is most important that the teacher continue to provide this reassurance throughout group work sessions. It is easy for students, in the middle of a frustrating work session, to blame themselves or others for the normal difficulties all people experience as they begin to work in groups. By modelling patient encouragement, and by articulating an understanding of the normal difficulties, teachers are able to help relieve student anxiety.

Teachers can also help provide a reassuring environment for their students by establishing safe and manageable opportunities for students to begin working together. Two ways many teachers do this is by keeping the group size very small and by helping students to develop positive working relationships.

Attending to Group Size

Many teachers prefer to begin with students in pairs. A group of two is very easily formed and invites the active participation of each partner. Working with one other person, in face-to-face interaction, provides a safe and manageable setting for most students inexperienced in group work. Most teachers recommend using pairs for an extended time and waiting until students are working productively before using larger groupings.

One gradual way to build the concept of working in a larger group is to ask each pair to "consult" with another pair after the initial work in pairs is complete. For example, dividing up the exercises to be done in mathematics and having partners check each other's work before "consulting" with another pair will save time and will allow the teacher to focus on problems that "consulting" pairs cannot resolve.

Beginning activities may also work well in groups of three and four members. Sometimes being in a group of three or four will seem safer than working in pairs, especially for students who are normally shy or quiet. A group of three or four provides more resources for discussion and enough opportunities for all members to contribute. The use of either pairs or larger groups will depend on the objectives for the activity, the nature of the task, and the personality of the students involved. *[handwritten: teacher decide]*

Building Working Relationships

One of the goals of getting started in small group work is to help students get to know one another and establish working relationships. To help students begin to know one another, teachers often provide opportunities for students, in groups, to respond personally to the topic of study. This creates relevance. It also builds working relationships because students share their personal experience and current thinking.

If there are negative social dynamics in the classroom it is difficult for students to focus on academic content in group work. Teachers develop different strategies to deal with this situation.

Some teachers plan academic content which is new and intriguing, or which is likely to be easily enjoyed. Social relationships improve when the academic task is engaging and non-threatening. Success in accomplishing the academic task promotes positive feelings among group members.

Sometimes teachers may plan group-building activities or games to establish rapport. There are many books which contain examples of such activities, including team quizzes, puzzles, co-operative games, and problem-solving activities. These activities provide a different focus from the regular class experience and allow students to learn dimensions about themselves and others which may not be elicited when doing conventional academic work. Learning about others helps students build mutual respect and mutual interest.

Sample Activities for Building Working Relationships

Getting Acquainted

If students are working in new groups, take some time for group members to learn other members' names and a little about each other. One simple way to do this is for each member to introduce him/herself and share a thought on one of the following questions or other questions selected by the teacher or the group:

- a particular interest he/she has;
- a place where he/she feels really happy and why;
- a place he/she would like to visit and why;
- a person he/she really admires and why;
- an initial viewpoint on the topic to be studied;
- an initial question about the topic to be studied.

Introducing Partners

Members can pair within their groups of four. Each partner interviews the other for three minutes using one or more questions such as the ones above. Then group members take turns introducing their partners to the other members of the group.

Personal Response

If groups are working together for a number of class periods the initial few minutes of each work session might be devoted to personal discussion. Discussion can be stimulated by a quick comment from each group member regarding such issues as the following:

- a personal reaction to the last period's discussion, reading, or topic;
- a hope of this period's group work;
- a personal application of the work being done;
- thoughts since last time;
- a quick report on how the assignment is coming and any problems with it.

Thoughts About the Topic of Study

Questions such as the following ask students to share their thoughts regarding the subject under consideration.

- Which character in the story would you rather be? Why?
- If this subject, issue, problem were an animal, what kind of animal would it be? List three characteristics of that animal.
- Would you be willing to have your use of television restricted at home to conserve fossil fuel?
- Do you agree or disagree with a decision made by a character in the story? Why?

Giving students a few minutes to think about the answer and to jot notes is helpful before students offer their initial comments.

Observing Students to Generate New Understandings

Small group work is an ideal setting for teachers to learn from and about their students. Teachers provide carefully structured opportunities for students to work together and then observe the classroom interaction. Patient, sensitive watching and listening provide teachers with rich possibilities for understanding how students are thinking and feeling and how the group work is developing. Gradually, teachers build the knowledge and confidence to intervene appropriately to support individuals and groups in their learning.

Through observation, teachers are able to gather information which will form the basis for making decisions about modifying, extending, or reshaping the group activities. For example, the teacher may notice many students talking together at the beginning of group work before starting on the task. Through closer observation, or by interviewing students, the teacher can make inferences about the nature of such talk. It may be that the requirements of the task are unclear and the teacher may intervene by writing a list of the requirements on the chalkboard. It may be that the students are talking to explore their understanding of the assigned question before working on possible answers. In this second case, the teacher may wish to comment on the importance of such talk in whole class discussion. Further, the teacher may set aside time at the beginning of the next small group work session for groups to explore and clarify the meaning of the question before discussing possible answers.

Thoughtful observation provides the teacher with the most direct source for understanding students' needs in starting group work. For further ideas on observation and intervention, teachers can refer to Chapter Six.

Building in Reflection
Right from the Start

Providing students with regular opportunities to learn about the process of working together is an important part of helping students get started in group work. Teachers can develop questions to help students reflect on their experience working in groups. Questions for this type of reflection may be as simple as, "How does your group deal with interruptions when you're working?" or "What things did you do in your group that made the group work well together?" or "What one thing could your group do better?"

Teachers can raise questions which are appropriate to the needs, developmental stages, and interests of their students. For example, students in early adolescence may benefit by thinking about ways to encourage others to express ideas and opinions, whereas six-year-olds may need to think about ways of helping others without domineering.

One simple way to help students reflect is to brainstorm a list of positives and a list of wishes, or concerns, on a chart such as the following:

Example of One Group's Reflection

About Our Group Work

Positives	Wishes/Concerns
• Everyone participated.	• We wish we got started faster.
• We stayed on task.	• We wish that only one person talked at a time.
• We all helped one another.	
• Everyone understands the work.	
• We organized our work folder well.	

Reflecting on their experiences of working in a group enables students to assess how their group worked and how they personally contributed. It helps them to develop an understanding about working with others, to learn and become aware of skills, and to set goals for the next group work session.

At the beginning of the next group work session the teacher asks students to review their goals and work toward them. This session offers students the opportunity to apply their new understanding. Practice then provides experience for further reflection.

same cycle teachers use to learn the best approaches to teaching their class

It is through repeated cycles of experience, reflection, understanding and practice that students learn co-operative skills. Reflection is a key stage in the learning cycle. Throughout the learning cycle the teacher can intervene with individuals, groups, and the whole class to provide support and information. Following is a description of the learning cycle.

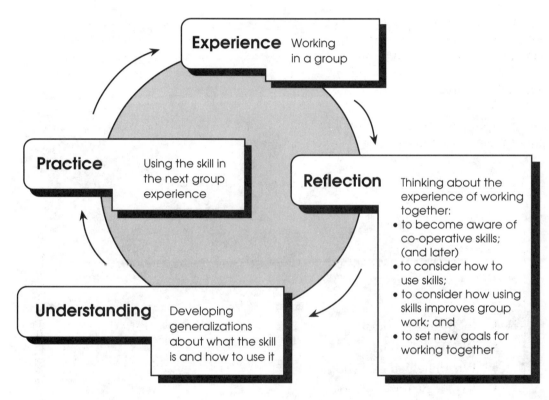

The above learning cycle is based on Kolb's experiential learning theory. See D. Kolb and R. Fry, "Towards an Applied Theory of Experiential Learning," in *Theories of Group Processes*, edited by C. Cooper (London: John Wiley, 1975); D. Kolb and L. Lewis, "Facilitating Experiential Learning: Observation and Reflection," in *Experiential and Simulation Techniques for Teaching Adults*, edited by L. Lewis (San Francisco: Jossey-Bass, 1986).

By building in reflection right from the start, teachers are structuring opportunities for students to think and talk about their experiences and therefore actively learn the skills helpful to effective group functioning.

As students learn co-operative skills, they feel more in command of their own participation and more able to influence others in positive directions. Students grow to enjoy working together, to care about each other's learning and to produce a high quality of work.

For further investigation of reflective activities and the teaching of co-operative skills, teachers can refer to Chapter Five.

Designing Beginning Group Activities

Teachers and students can ease gently into group work to allow themselves time to build trust and confidence in working together. Instant success in group work is rare. Both teachers and students should expect to encounter some awkward moments in the beginning. However, by moving slowly, starting with short and simple tasks and gradually increasing the complexity and length of the group activities, teachers can provide secure opportunities for everyone involved to become comfortable and productive with group work.

Some teachers find it helpful to start group work using familiar subject material. Teachers can also choose a time of day that is productive for group interaction. For example, some teachers find the morning a good time. By contrast, other teachers like the end of the day because group interaction is a way of energizing their students. Teachers on a rotary timetable may choose a class with which they have a comfortable rapport and wait until they feel more at ease to start with other classes. Teachers discover many ways to make their first experiences with groups successful for themselves and their students.

Beginning Group Activities

Start with Simple Tasks
- short (2-3 min.)
- specific
- concrete
- immediately relevant/purposeful

Keep the Groups Small
- pairs (often the safest beginning)
- threes and fours

Gradually Incorporate Group Activities Into Classroom Experience
- as an introduction to a lesson (for example, contributing personal knowledge related to the topic)
- as "pause for thought" during a lesson (for example, brainstorming questions)
- as a summary (for example, reviewing key ideas and vocabulary from a lesson)

There is often a belief among students, based on their past experience with ineffective group work, that work done in groups does not count and does not contribute to academic learning. From the very beginning, group activities should be linked clearly to the everyday learning of subject matter. In addition, they should help students and teachers develop comfort and expertise in group work.

Designing beginning group activities involves both planning the group tasks and the group interaction. The following suggestions help make students' initial experience with small groups both purposeful and well structured.

Suggestions for Planning Group Tasks

As a general rule beginning group activities should be short, as short as two or three minutes. In addition, the tasks should be kept specific and immediately purposeful.

Tasks Involving Mutual Exchange

These tasks are planned as an extension of work which students have prepared individually. Each student brings his/her work or ideas to contribute to the small group:

- checking a partner's understanding of directions for the assigned task;
- coaching each other through the steps of a task;
- trading initial responses to a film or story;
- comparing or combining each other's answers/homework;
- reviewing/drilling materials;
- reading each other's notes.

Sharing contributions demonstrates to students the potential of each class member to contribute and receive academic peer support.

Tasks Involving Exploratory Talk

Teachers can plan tasks which encourage the type of tentative, sometimes hesitant, exploratory talk necessary to allow students to make sense of new information. These tasks are planned to encourage students to talk through ideas, such as:

eg, pairing for computer assistance

- explaining to a partner:
  - a procedure demonstrated
  - a technical term just mentioned
  - reasons for a prediction/hypothesis
  - the meaning of a story title;
- relating a personal experience in response to an idea presented;
- working with new vocabulary (cloze exercises, sentence completion in groups);
- identifying the key points in a lesson;
- brainstorming possible answers to a question;
- verbalizing steps in a process.

These opportunities demonstrate to students that talk is a fundamental part of the learning process. Students learn to value talk as a way to enrich their own understanding. They learn to believe in their role of active participant in the learning process.

Peer group talk is especially important for students whose native language is not standard Canadian English. These students have an enormous task in assimilating new concepts through a new language. Peer tutors can help as these students talk through their ideas.

Tasks Involving Reshaping and Reorganizing Information

Students can work in small groups to reshape and reorganize information in activities, such as:

- developing questions on a topic;
- searching for or predicting patterns;
- generating hypotheses;
- brainstorming alternatives and consequences;
- comparing points of view;
- devising categories;
- making inferences and forecasting future events;
- making deductions from information given;
- elaborating on information to make it more interesting or useful;
- distinguishing fact from opinion;
- deciding what caused an event to occur;
- discussing steps and strategies for solving a problem.

These sessions provide students with opportunities to apply higher-level thinking skills. By working with others, students build a level of understanding that they cannot usually achieve independently.

Through these three types of group activities — mutual exchange, exploratory talk, and re-shaping information — students realize their individual potential to contribute in a shared learning setting. Students grow to understand the value of talking to learn. Additionally, students begin to perceive the power of collaboration in relation to their own learning.

Suggestions for Planning Group Interaction

The following six suggestions illustrate simple ways that discussion within groups can be structured to help students learn to work productively together:

- Ground Rules;
- Preparing Individual Contributions Ahead of Time;
- Guidelines for Brainstorming;
- Structuring Response;
- Numbering Off;
- Assigning Roles.

Ground Rules

Teachers may provide guidelines at the beginning of the year to assist students in learning how to work productively in groups. For example, the following three rules suggested by Carol Meyer and Tom Sallee in their book *Make it Simpler, A Practical Guide To Problem Solving in Mathematics* (Addison-Wesley, 1983) are helpful.

1. You are responsible for your own contribution and behaviour.
2. You must be willing to help any group member who asks.
3. You may ask for help from the teacher only when no one in your group can answer your question.

Preparing Individual Contributions Ahead of Time

Students prepare by working alone to make some notes that organize their current thinking so they will have something specific to contribute. All opening statements are tabled before any discussion occurs; each person takes a turn to speak about the topic without being interrupted. Then the group discussion takes place. The teacher signals the groups when the time for discussion is almost over. At this point, time is provided for each person to make a summary comment before the class reconvenes.

Guidelines for Brainstorming

Brainstorming is a useful way of generating a large number of alternative ideas for discussion and evaluation. Brainstorming works best when students employ the following guidelines.

- There should be no evaluation of ideas until after the brainstorming session.
- Quantity is more important than quality. Get as many ideas as possible within a given time limit.
- Expand on others' ideas; if someone else's idea prompts another in your mind, share it.
- Zany ideas are welcome.
- Record all ideas.

Structuring Response

One highly structured way to help students listen actively and engage in discussion is to provide each group member with the opportunity for making one comment or asking one question in response to the opening statement of each group member. For example, in a group of three, after group member one makes his/her opening statement, group member two and three are given an opportunity to respond. Then group member two makes his/her opening statement and group members one and three respond. The opportunity for every student to make a comment or ask a question helps encourage active listening and responding — vital functions for productive discussion.

Numbering Off

Students in the group count off to identify the order in which they will speak. This strategy works well in situations where students are making lists, for example, a list of initial individual responses, a list of questions, a list of possible solutions, or a list of numbers in sequence. Numbering off helps students to participate without the management difficulty of deciding who goes first and who goes last. Numbering off helps to equalize participation so that everyone has a turn.

Assigning Roles

Good beginning

Teachers may assign roles which help get the work done in the group. Roles, such as recorder, reporter, and time keeper help organize and facilitate the participation of group members. Roles can be assigned easily by number. For example, when students have numbered off, the teacher can announce that member number one will be responsible for reporting briefly at the conclusion of the discussion. If participation is sequentially ordered, the role of time keeper is most suitably given to the member with the last number . . . this person has a vested interest in keeping the discussion moving.

Other kinds of roles, such as those which structure the actual discussion, may be assigned. Roles such as "interviewer," "guest panelist," and "chair" help students to make contributions by virtue of their specialization. Role cards like the ones below are helpful.

CHECKER

Check to make sure that everyone agrees with the answer and that everyone understands the work.

ENCOURAGER

Encourage others to share ideas, to give opinions or to help others. Also, encourage the group to work hard.

In some classes students will begin to work productively without the assistance of structures such as those described above. These suggestions may be most helpful at the beginning of group work, and afterwards used only on an occasional basis to renew understanding of co-operative group interaction.

A classroom which includes frequent opportunities for students to work productively in small groups will produce an inviting learning environment. As the composition of pairs or groups of three and four changes, students have opportunities to work closely with and get to know personally many members of their class. This interaction builds a sense of unity within the class, while honouring the diversity and unique talents of each individual. Gradually, through experience and reflection, students come to work in an atmosphere of mutual respect. This co-operative environment offers rich support as the teacher begins to organize longer and larger group tasks.

Informing Parents

Parents also need to understand the purposes and benefits of co-operative small group learning. Parents and students' own educational experiences in Canada and elsewhere have shaped their expectations of school and of instructional practice. People who have experienced teacher-centred approaches to education may need additional time and opportunities to understand the very different approach to learning that interactive and co-operative small group learning advocates.

The following pages provide sample information for parents. Teachers will want to personalize communication by choosing information which is relevant to the interests of parents in their community.

Sample Information for Parents

In co-operative small group learning students collaborate to learn together. These methods of group work are significantly different from traditional methods of group work. Each student feels responsible and accountable for working hard to accomplish the academic task.

The amount of time teachers use co-operative small group learning in their classrooms varies. It is likely that a teacher might use these methods approximately 25-30% of the time. Group work is appropriate for many learning activities. Teachers also use whole-class and independent approaches where these are appropriate for effective student learning.

The effectiveness of co-operative small group learning is supported by a solid body of research evidence including over 800 studies. The research demonstrates that students develop higher individual academic achievement, stronger feelings of self-worth, and more positive attitudes toward others, toward learning, and toward school.

Teachers appreciate the enthusiasm and energy for learning which small group work generates among students. There are greater opportunities for students:

- to become actively involved in learning and to develop greater motivation to learn;
- to develop positive attitudes toward subject matter;
- to practise higher-level thinking skills;
- to develop caring and respect for self and others;
- to accept responsibility and learn self-discipline.

Teachers enjoy the very active teaching roles provided by co-operative small group learning. There are greater opportunities for teachers:

- to get to know students through observation and small group discussion;
- to interact frequently and on personal terms with all students;
- to meet the individual needs of students through greater flexibility;
- to offer students personalized support and challenges;
- to build a classroom environment which is highly supportive of learning;
- to address the academic, social and personal development of students.

Students enjoy being actively involved in their learning. Student appreciate the supportive and positive attitudes which their classmates exhibit toward learning. There are greater opportunities for students:

- to feel competent, able to achieve, and able to learn;
- to feel a sense of belonging, of being accepted and supported by classmates;

- to feel responsible for their learning and behaviour in the class and school;
- to feel positively toward teachers and school.

Parents whose children have worked with teachers who incorporate co-operative small groups into their classroom programs are very supportive. Perhaps the strongest reason parents like co-operative small group methods is that teachers are able to focus intently on the academic subject while fostering the personal and social development of their students. Parents see this as a productive use of time, and every student is able to gain maximum benefit.

Additionally, parents feel very strongly that their children should learn skills which will be required in their future occupations. Parents want their children to be able to work productively with others, to solve problems, collaborate to create new knowledge, work hard as a member of a team, care about the quality of everyone's work, and become good citizens. Parents know that their children will enter a demanding work force where professions, businesses, industries, and the arts increasingly rely upon their members to work productively with others.

Parents also appreciate the ways in which co-operative small group work fosters the development of higher-level thinking skills in all students. Not only will these skills contribute to success in the world of work, but also they will help students meet the complex challenges of social and family life.

Parents whose children work in co-operative small groups understand how the supportive and nurturing academic learning environment helps individuals become self-directed and self-motivated learners.

Summary

By providing rationale and reassurance, by observing and reflecting, by structuring beginning activities carefully, and by informing parents, teachers can organize secure and practical ways for students to begin co-operative small group learning.

A classroom which includes frequent opportunities for students to work productively in small groups will create an inviting learning environment. As the composition of partners or groups of three and four changes, students have opportunities to work closely with and get to know personally many members of their class. Gradually, through experience and reflection, students come to work in an atmosphere of mutual respect and trust. This co-operative environment offers rich support as the teacher begins to organize longer and more complex group tasks.

3 Five Kinds of Groups

When I started I was very shy and didn't say much in a group. I didn't think anybody would listen or care. Now I can talk in a group even if others disagree with me, and I've learned how to listen to others.

Truong, Grade 6

Successful co-operative learning activities are dependent upon an interplay of these five principles.

1. Students work in positive interdependence.

2. Students work in small heterogeneous groups.

3. Students are accountable both as individuals and as a group.

4. Students learn through ample opportunity for purposeful talk.

5. Students learn and practise co-operative skills as they study and explore the subject matter together.

These principles are introduced in Chapter One and included as part of discussion in Chapter Two. Chapters Three and Four demonstrate how the principles work in practical application. Chapters Five and Six provide information on the teaching of co-operative skills. Chapter Seven describes evaluation methods.

The more complex the task, the more useful co-operative learning is — it saves the teacher having to repeat explanations. The students help each other learn the concepts.

Elementary Teacher

It's exciting to see the dialogue going on between the students in small groups. They clue into ideas that might not come out in a lesson where the focus is on what I have to say.

Secondary Teacher

 I can cover more work using co-operative learning. The children enjoy it and learn more from it — they learn about questions they want answers to, rather than only listening to what I tell them.

Elementary Teacher

Five Kinds of Groups

This chapter introduces five kinds of co-operative small groups:

- informal groups;
- base groups;
- combined groups;
- reconstituted groups;
- representative groups.

The five kinds of groups are broadly generic and encompass a variety of groupings described in other co-operative learning resources. Each of the five kinds of groups may be used to accomplish many different learning objectives. Two or more of the five kinds may be put together in various ways as building blocks to create expanded small group learning experiences.

Teachers may wish to skim the chapter and then select one of the five kinds of groups to investigate initially. Experimenting with all five groups at once may result in frustration for both teacher and students. By moving slowly and concentrating on one kind of group, the teacher and students will develop comfort and confidence. Of the five group types, informal groups are probably most familiar to teachers.

As teacher and students become familiar with one kind of group, the many possibilities for variation and modification will become evident. Likewise, as teachers and students become familiar with the other four kinds of groups, the possibilities for combinations and extensions of the five building blocks will develop naturally.

Initially, teachers may find that they are spending more time and effort in preparing materials and designing learning activities than they were before. But this increased work load soon lessens and, in time, teachers report that they are easily able to incorporate group work in both planned and spontaneous ways. Teachers enjoy the ability to use the different kinds of groups creatively. In a short time they are able to judge which kind of grouping is most appropriate in particular situations.

There is a lot more involved in making group work effective than knowing what kind of grouping is most appropriate in specific situations. Teachers also need to know about the teaching of co-operative skills, elements of the teacher's role, and evaluation. Information on these topics can be found in Chapters Five, Six, and Seven.

This handbook contains examples for each of the grade levels. Teachers may see ways to adapt some examples for use in lower or higher grade levels. Many examples in this chapter can also be adapted for use in other contexts, such as adult education, including staff development.

Informal Groups

The purpose of an informal group is to provide students with an immediate forum for talking. Teachers create these groups by asking students to turn to those seated closest and "put their heads together."

Informal groups can meet for as little as two minutes or for as long as twenty minutes. Informal groups can be used anytime during a presentation. At the beginning of a lesson students can talk in these groups to elicit personal relevance, to assess current knowledge, to raise questions, and to generate interest in a new topic. At the end, students can talk in these groups to summarize, review, analyze information, or brainstorm new questions.

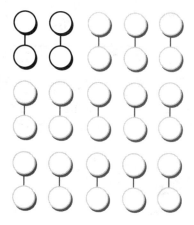

Discussion in small groups is also useful during presentations. The teacher may pause at appropriate moments to ask informal groups, for example, to list the last three points, to clarify the two issues presented, or to identify the main idea. Occasionally, informal discussion groups may work continuously throughout a class session, with the teacher reconvening the class two or three times by asking for quick reports or answers to questions posed.

In informal groups students can clarify and expand upon information as well as check ideas with peers before contributing to the whole class. Often this discussion provides a filter and/or support for ideas which otherwise would not be dealt with in the class discussion. Informal groups also provide students with freedom to think out loud without the pressure of a large audience. Informal exchange is an effective way to encourage the use of students' thinking skills: describing how they completed a task, relating ideas to their own experience, and understanding others' ideas and approaches.

Many teachers prefer a group size of between two and four members. A group of two is very easily formed and ensures active participation by each partner. A group of three or four provides more resources for discussion and enough opportunities for all members to contribute. A group of more than four takes longer to form and requires more formality. For example, a chairperson is usually needed to facilitate the active involvement of members.

Four Uses of Informal Groups

Guided Practice

After the teacher demonstrates an activity, students in pairs take turns manipulating equipment or practising a technique. The roles of supervisor and technician may be assigned as students coach each other through the process. In the role of technician, the student will talk out what he/she is doing and why; in the role of supervisor, the partner will verbalize confirmation.

Sample Activities

Computers

The teacher has posted the steps for starting up and closing down a computer program beside the classroom computer. The students practise in pairs to become familiar with the process, talking each other through the steps.

Family Studies

The teacher demonstrates how to thread a bobbin. Students then practise in pairs, talking through what they are doing.

French

The teacher has role played a situation in which someone makes a phone call and leaves a message. Pairs of students are provided with a script for the person answering the phone. One partner reads from the script while the other improvises responses. Students then reverse roles.

Keyboarding

The teacher has taught the steps involved in tabulating. Students work in pairs, taking turns to talk one another through the process and to practise.

Brainstorming

Brainstorming is a useful way of generating a large number of alternative ideas for discussion and evaluation. As mentioned in Chapter Two, brainstorming works best when students employ the following guidelines.

1. There should be no evaluation of ideas until after the brainstorming session.
2. Quantity is more important than quality. Get as many ideas as possible within a given time limit.
3. Expand on others' ideas; if someone else's idea prompts another in your mind, share it.
4. Zany ideas are welcome.
5. Record all ideas.

Brainstorming begins with the teacher posing an open-ended question. Students work to generate and record a list of alternative ideas. Following brainstorming, the teacher asks a question to assist the students in sorting or evaluating their list of ideas.

Sample Topics and Questions for Brainstorming

School Concerns

List ways we could welcome people when they enter our building. Which activities could students do without the teacher's assistance?

English

List strategies you have found helpful in making revisions. Which strategy might you try first? Why?

Family Studies

List all the things which parents owe children. Place an E beside things you think are easy to provide and an H for things which are hard to provide.

Geography

Look at the map of the proposed town plan. List all the possible uses for the piece of vacant land in map section C-4. Which uses are the most appropriate? Why?

Math

Find all the ways to write the numbers from 1 to 25 as the sum of consecutive numbers. Look for patterns in your list.

Social Studies

A pioneer family has arrived at a new and heavily wooded site with a limited supply of food. How will the family meet its food needs for the next two weeks? Which ways will require co-operation among family members? Why?

Response Discussion

Response discussions provide opportunities for students in small groups to respond personally to an idea, event, issue or topic. These discussions enable students to air their views and to feel "heard."

Sample Topics

School Concerns

- the assembly this morning
- yesterday's field trip
- the new rule about throwing snowballs
- sponsoring a foster child
- how your group worked together yesterday

Career Awareness
things you learned which you didn't expect to learn from the job shadowing work experience

English
the film we just viewed

French
the role play you just performed

Math
what you do or don't understand about tessellations

Science
the concerns expressed in the editorial of the daily newspaper regarding local air or water pollution

Quick Reports

Students can report to each other about the work they are doing individually.

Sample Topics

Art
how you planned your design

Math
strategies you found successful for solving problems

Music
the organization of your personal practice time

Technological Studies
progress report on your project

Base Groups

The primary purpose of base groups is to encourage long-term peer support for learning. These groups of two, three, or four students are carefully formed by the teacher and are designed to stay together for a long period, perhaps the whole term or semester. Teachers often wait to form these groups until they become acquainted with their students. This helps the teacher to form socially and academically heterogeneous groups whose members will be able to build satisfying, long-term relationships.

It is important that the teacher carefully structure the composition of groups for both heterogeneity and compatibility. Heterogeneity of ethnicity, gender, ability, personality, and background brings diverse perspectives and talents to the group. As students work together over time they develop understanding, appreciation, and respect for others who seem different from themselves. Students learn to support and care for those students they may not otherwise come to know.

Teachers may modify the heterogeneity of groups by building on an element that group members have in common. For example, forming base groups to include a common academic interest, such as sectional groups in an instrumental music ensemble, provides an otherwise heterogeneous group with a common bond and a shared focus.

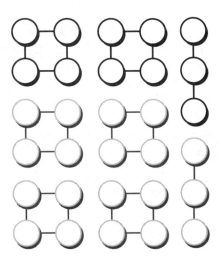

The teacher may also form base groups composed of students who feel comfortable with each other. This bond may be especially important in situations where many students in the classroom feel insecure or are easily upset or provoked. The teacher may use a questionnaire to ask students to identify three or four other students they would feel comfortable working with and then form pairs based on the information. After students have developed confidence from the experience of many successful base group activities, the teacher can build more heterogeneity in the groups.

In terms of students' personal and social development, base groups provide structured opportunities for all students to gain a sense of belonging and to develop respect and caring for themselves and others. Students learn to get along with others, to resolve conflicts, to contribute to the well-being of classmates and to develop new friendships.

In terms of students' academic development, base groups provide structured opportunities for students to articulate their own learning, receive feedback from peers, offer support to others' efforts, and share information and ideas. As the members of a group grow to trust and respect one another, a base group builds peer sanction for academic effort and offers a supportive environment to discuss academic challenges.

Initially teachers provide clear guidelines for base group meeting agendas and the responsibilities of members to one another. Once students become familiar with base groups, they readily assume responsibility and establish their own group guidelines.

Because they stay together over long periods of time, base groups offer an ideal setting for students to learn co-operative skills. Through cycles of working together, reflecting and setting new goals, students build the trust level within their group, become comfortable with each other, and support each others' efforts to work together effectively.

Teachers who group students in squads in physical education; teams in math, science or computer labs; or work groups in family and technological studies will be forming effective base groups if the emphasis is on the learning of co-operative skills. Suggestions for teaching co-operative skills are provided in Chapter Five.

Two Uses for Base Groups

① Coaching

A coaching group provides a supportive place for students to help each other master subject matter. Students may tutor one another in learning the steps of a process, drill basic facts, review a unit of study, guide each other's practice of skills, check each other's notes, discuss and compare homework, or co-operatively take a test.

Samples of Coaching Activities

Homework Checks

A grade eight language and reading teacher forms groups of four students to help each other with homework concerns. Groups meet to brainstorm lists of ways they could support one another. The teacher provides a few minutes of meeting time on a consistent basis when homework is assigned. On long projects the teacher arranges periodic "check" sessions for groups to meet. Students exchange home phone numbers, arrange to work at the same time during the evening when a group member requests phone "check-ins," and set goals together for personal improvement.

Proofing Notes

A grade seven science class develops a co-operative summary of good science notebook practices. By categorizing practices and coding them, the class develops improvement code symbols for partners to use. The teacher forms coaching pairs where partners are responsible for reading each other's notes and for using the coding symbols to make suggestions for improvement. Notes are corrected and submitted to the teacher.

Study Groups

The teacher forms groups of four students to divide up daily homework questions in calculus. Each class begins with the students working in study groups to review the problem-solving process for the homework questions they did individually. The group members work together to help one another solve problems which caused difficulties. The teacher reviews questions which the groups could not solve collaboratively.

Understanding Directions

A second-language teacher forms coaching pairs where partners are responsible, throughout the term, for talking through and understanding the directions for assignments before individual students proceed to work. The teacher introduces vocabulary for giving help and asking questions in the second language to help students communicate in their coaching relationship. Pairs also turn to each other for assistance in working on assignments before requesting help from the teacher.

② Collaborating

In a collaborative group, students meet together on a regular basis to articulate personal learning goals, offer encouragement and academic support, and discuss their individual progress. Following are examples of activities for collaborative base groups.

- Students meet to discuss the progress of individual portfolios.
- Students engaged in independent research projects voice problems at regular group meetings and brainstorm alternative solutions.
- Students meet on a regular basis to share response journals during the independent reading of a novel.
- Students in lab teams or technical crews meet to review safety guidelines and machine maintenance, and role play simulated emergencies.
- Students bring favourite or interesting passages from books or articles to read to one another on a biweekly basis in a reading council group.
- Students schedule conference meetings with their writing group members as they require support in various stages of writing, and meet weekly to share writing from their writing folders.

Samples of Collaborating Activities

Portfolio Groups
Students in a business class collect daily samples of their work in a portfolio file. The teacher sets aside time on a weekly basis for portfolio groups to meet. At the beginning of the semester, the teacher formally structures tasks for the portfolio group to accomplish. Students list academic and personal learning goals to share in their portfolio group. On a weekly basis students bring their work for discussion. They note common concerns and brainstorm strategies for improving their work. Occasionally, the teacher identifies a general issue for discussion by all of the portfolio groups. Over the course of the semester, the groups learn to set the meeting agenda for themselves. Portfolio groups can also be used in other subjects in which students keep portfolios of their work, for example, studio art, creative writing, science lab experiments, math problem solving.

Classroom Support Groups
The teacher establishes support groups of three or four students who will meet together many times over the year to work on a variety of activities. The teacher selects activities which will foster a sense of caring and support among the group members. During the "becoming acquainted" phase, these groups will often create a name and logo for themselves.

The following list represents some of the many activities that teachers create for classroom support groups:

- solving classroom problems;
- planning class parties and events;
- planning class excursions, travelling together, and working on follow-up activities;
- attending assemblies together and holding response discussions;
- discussing weekly personal selection of library books;
- sharing a work space and organizing that space;
- planning and making bulletin boards and special displays;
- taking on the class jobs together as a team for a monthly period;
- meeting together on a weekly basis to reflect on, discuss, and write an evaluation of the week;
- working together on a special project to share with the class;
- being responsible for "catch up" — collecting materials and phoning information when a member is absent;
- forming study teams for tests, upgrading, and catching up.

Combined Groups

The primary purpose of combined small groups is to provide opportunities for groups to help each other learn through a consultative process. Combined groups are formed when two or more groups bring their work to a meeting together.

Combinations may be random or based on the proximity of groups. However, combinations may also be based on shared interest or perspective. Decisions to combine may be made by students or combinations may be assigned by the teacher.

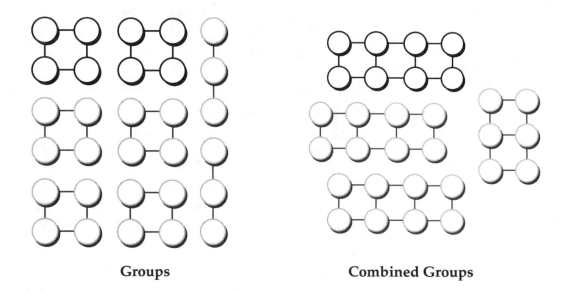

Groups   Combined Groups

Combined groups help at any stage of a learning task. For example, groups may consult during an initial planning stage to define a problem, establish research questions, discuss procedures for accomplishing the work, list criteria for success, or consider the presentation format.

Groups can meet together during tasks to compare work, share expertise, or generate a collective data base. Combined groups also offer an efficient forum for groups to present their work, thereby freeing the class from the tedium of serial small-group-to-whole-class presentations.

Combined group meetings are usually short, occurring as a subtask within the context of a larger task. These meetings may last from 10 to 30 minutes, depending on the purpose of the meeting. Sometimes combined groups "snowball" to meet with other combined groups. A description of "snowballing" is provided in Chapter Four.

Three Uses of Combined Groups

Building Information/Expertise

When two groups combine to share information and expertise both benefit. The following sample activities encourage use of thinking skills, such as posing questions, giving reasons for opinions, classifying information while the students are sharing information.

Sample Activities

Business English
Pairs read an article on communication skills. They brainstorm two lists — one of nonverbal messages which invite communication and one of nonverbal messages which discourage communication. Each pair meets with another pair to make a chart which combines their lists.

Co-operative Skills
Each group identifies three characteristics of an effective group. Two groups combine to make one collective list.

Language
Writing pairs brainstorm a list in response to the following question, "If you had a pile of stories, and you were going to divide them into two piles — stories you like and stories you don't like — how would they be different?" Pairs combine to make one collective list.

Math
Groups of two try ten experiments as part of a probability study. Two groups meet to combine the results, effectively doubling the number of experiments.

Science
The class is about to begin a study of photosynthesis. Each group lists three things members think they know about photosynthesis and one question they have. Groups combine to put their lists together.

② Analyzing Information

Two groups can combine their work to compare and analyze information.

Sample Activities

Language
Each student has brought a stuffed toy to school. Pairs work together to generate a list of questions to interview a stuffed toy. Pairs combine to compare the questions on their lists.

Math
Students work in pairs to answer ten questions. One partner does the odd-numbered questions and one does the even-numbered questions. Partners check each other's work so they can agree on the answers to the ten questions. Then they combine with another group to compare answers and work out discrepancies. The combined groups report to the teacher on solutions involving disagreement.

Preparing for Open House
The class is responsible for preparing the classroom for Open House. Each group is designing a different display. Combined groups compare designs and get helpful comments. Each group then works alone to revise its plan before submitting it to the teacher.

Science
Groups of three are devising experiments to test the hypothesis that all forms of paper towel absorb the same amount of water per unit cost. Groups combine to analyze their experiments and findings in the light of the hypothesis.

③ Reporting/Presenting

There are a number of ways to avoid the tedium of a long series of small-group-to-whole-class presentations. One way is to combine two or three groups to present to each other. Each presentation can be followed by questions and discussion.

Sample Activities

English
Each group of three reads and talks about a different novel related to the same topic or theme. Groups combine to give book reports.

History
The class is studying Chamberlain's appeasement policy. Different groups are building a case for and against appeasement. Groups combine to debate their conflicting viewpoints.

Problem Solving
The class is studying an approach to problem solving. Each group uses the approach to solve a problem. The problem could be related to classroom concerns, current news topics, subject-specific topics in math, technological studies, office management, law, family studies, parenting, world politics, and so on. Groups combine to report both on solutions and on the effectiveness of the problem-solving method.

Reconstituted Groups

The primary purpose of reconstituted groups is to provide opportunities for students to gain a diversity of perspectives and insights by participating in both a home group and a cross group. Reconstituted groups offer students quick access to a broad base of information because they provide opportunity to talk with a larger number of people.

Reconstituted groups are formed by placing students in a home group and a cross group. First, students work on a topic in a home group, then move to a different group to explore a particular subtopic, idea, theme, issue, or question related to the topic. Students return to the home group, bringing back information from their work in the cross grouping.

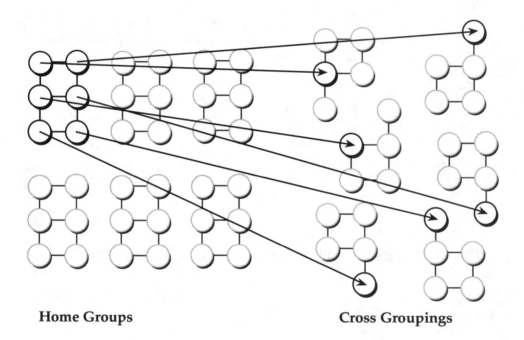

Home Groups   **Cross Groupings**

Cross groupings can be very simply formed by numbering off in the home groups. All the one's form one cross group, the two's another, and so on. Alternatively, students can be asked to find someone in another home group to work with.

Reconstituted groups can also be formally structured by the teacher. To do this the teacher can design a grid such as the one shown on p. 57.

By moving names about in the grid the teacher can ensure an appropriate mix of students by ethnicity, gender, ability, personality, and background in both the home groups (lettered) and the cross groups (numbered).

	A	B	C	D	E
1	Satinder	Derek	Cathy	Duc	Peter
2	Kiran	Susan	Michael	Julie	Tania
3	Patricia	Aly	Sonia	Andre	Tony
4	Matthew	Beenu	Sanjay	Nayoung	Mari
5	Maneesh	Kristen	Juan	Pyrha	Petula
6	Erin	Jaghit	Michele	Daniel	Angela

The composition of the home and cross groups will depend upon the purposes and criteria established by the teacher or, in some cases, by the students. Sometimes, for certain purposes, the cross groups may be homogeneous interest groups. The teacher may also arrange cross groups to accommodate different learning styles or needs of students. For example, all the students in one cross group may benefit from extra support in second-language acquisition. All the students in another cross group may learn more easily using nonprint resources.

Jigsaw is one highly successful way of using reconstituted groups. In the literature on Jigsaw, the cross groups are referred to either as exploration groups or expert groups. There are two general versions of Jigsaw. In "JIGSAW 1" the exploration groups work on different subtopics related to the topic as a whole. In "JIGSAW 2" the exploration groups work on the same topic but explore the same topic from different perspectives. Following is a general outline of how the strategy works and examples of both uses. Once the Jigsaw structure is understood, teachers find it interesting to develop their own variations.

The Jigsaw Strategy

Students work together in small groups and must rely on each other. Each member explores subtopics in the subject matter and therefore possesses critical information to contribute to classmates. Co-operation and mutual trust become valuable and necessary to academic achievement. Following is an outline of the Jigsaw strategy.

① Step 1: Introduction

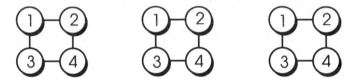

The teacher organizes the class into heterogeneous "home" groups. Each group member is given, or selects, a subtopic or theme which is part of the subject matter to be studied. As part of the introduction, the teacher and students discuss the objectives and evaluative activities for their learning. The teacher may involve the students in planning the evaluation activity.

② Step 2: Exploration

Students reorganize to form "exploration" groups. Members of each group work together to learn about their topic.

③ Step 3: Reporting/Reshaping

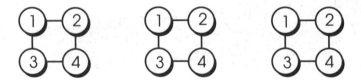

Students return to their home groups. Group members take turns presenting their subtopic or perspective.

④ Step 4: Integration/Evaluation

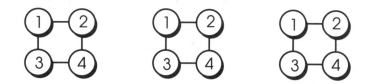

Students participate in an evaluation activity. As part of the evaluation, the teacher assists students to think about how well their groups worked together and about what they might do differently next time. The teacher may decide to involve students in an activity to teach co-operative skills. Information on the evaluation of co-operative learning is provided in Chapter Seven.

The Jigsaw Strategy is described by Elliot Aronson. See Elliot Aronson et. al., *The Jigsaw Classroom* (Beverley Hills, California: Sage, 1978).

The information and examples in this section are adapted from Judy Clarke and Ron Wideman, *Co-operative Learning - The Jigsaw Strategy* (Scarborough, Ontario: Scarborough Board of Education, The Values Education Project, 1985).

Two Uses of Jigsaw

Jigsaw I: Preparing for a Debate

Step 1: Introduction
The class is studying an issue to prepare for a debate which will be held later. The teacher has collected five articles presenting different sides of the issue.

The teacher organizes the class of 30 into six home groups of five members. Each member of each home group will explore one article in order to share the information with the other home group members. Each home group member selects his/her article.

Step 2: Exploration
Each exploration group of six members meets to discuss the article and to prepare notes. A group as large as six needs a chairperson to facilitate discussion. Alternatively, the teacher or the students may choose to subdivide each exploration group into two groups of three.

Step 3: Reporting/Reshaping
Students return to the home groups. Each member in each home group presents the information from his/her article. Discussion is encouraged within the group.

Step 4: Integration/Evaluation
The home group prepares a list of pro's and con's regarding the issue. The teacher collects all the ideas on a master chart. Each home group reports one idea in turn, until all ideas have been presented. Each home group hands in its list to the teacher. The class completes the Jigsaw with a five minute evaluation of how effectively the home group worked. Each group identifies two things which went well and one thing which the group would do differently next time.

NOTE:
The use of journal and newspaper articles and materials to explore an issue can be used by teachers across many grade levels and subject areas.

Jigsaw 1: Solving a School Problem

Step 1: Introduction
The class has been working on problem-solving strategies as part of a year-long learning objective. The school dance has been an upsetting event to many students. The teacher elicits a list of problems surrounding the dance, and students rank the top five problems.

The teacher organizes the class of 30 into six home groups of five. Each member of each home group selects one of the top five problems to solve in his/her exploration group.

Step 2: Exploration
Exploration groups meets to use a problem-solving model to explore the problem and develop a list of alternative solutions.

Step 3: Reporting/Reshaping
Each member in each home group describes the proposed solution developed by his/her exploration group and asks for questions and comments from other home group members.

Step 4: Integration/Evaluation
Exploration groups meet again. Members report the responses they received from students in their home groups. Solutions may then be revised. Each group presents its revised proposal to the class. Proposals are saved for review after the next school dance.

The teacher reports to the class about his observations on the developing use of co-operative skills. He asks groups to brainstorm positive ways to invite others to participate. The teacher records the groups' ideas and reviews them with the class at the beginning of the next group work activity. He asks students to practise the skill of inviting others to participate. For more information on this aspect of the teacher's role, see Chapter Six.

NOTE:
This example provides a variation to the Jigsaw model. In this case the exploration groups work together twice. The first time, exploration groups work to explore their problem and devise alternative solutions. The second time, they meet to revise solutions based on response from the home groups.

Jigsaw 2: Responding to a Video

Step 1: Introduction
The teacher organizes the class of 28 into home groups of three members. There are eight groups of three and one group of four. The teacher shows the video *What is Work?* and asks students to discuss their immediate responses in home groups. The teacher has developed three questions to explore the video. Each member of each home group selects one of the questions. In the group of four, two members "twin" to share one of the questions.

Step 2: Exploration
Students with the same question meet in a particular corner of the classroom to form exploration groups of two or three members. Each exploration group discusses its question.

Step 3: Reporting/Reshaping
Home groups meet. Each member reports on the discussion which took place in his/her exploration group.

Step 4: Integration/Evaluation
Each home group develops a five-point philosophy of work and creates a poster on construction paper using words or symbols to represent its five-point philosophy. These are posted at the front of the class. Each student fills out an evaluation form to analyze his/her contribution to working relationships in the groups. Chapter Five provides examples of such evaluation forms.

NOTE:
Classes don't have to divide evenly into multiples for Jigsaw to work. For example, the teacher can assign an additional student to some home groups. This student can "twin" with another student from the same group as they move into exploration groups. Alternatively, the teacher may ask some students to observe the groups working together, to identify positive patterns, and to report to the class during step four.

Jigsaw 2: Responding to an Article

Step 1: Introduction
The teacher introduces an article which will be read by the whole class. The class is organized into home groups and students are asked to work in these home groups to share their initial responses to the article.

Step 2: Exploration
The teacher has developed five questions to help students study the article. By numbering off, students are organized into exploration groups. Each exploration group discusses one of the questions.

Step 3: Reporting/Reshaping
Students return to their home groups and each member is responsible for sharing the key points discussed in his/her exploration group. Students are encouraged to ask questions of one another and to work to clarify issues. This stage usually leads to further discussion of each question.

Step 4: Integration/Evaluation
Students write individually in their journals or notebooks to express their own point of view in the light of the shared perspectives and discussions.

NOTE:
The example above can be adapted to explore many different kinds of material and shared experiences such as media presentations, dramatic presentations, lectures, stories, films, as well as excursions.

Representative Groups

The primary purpose of representative groups is to provide a forum for discussion on the work of groups within the class. For example, the discussion may involve a presentation from each group representative, progress reports on group work, problem solving, or the co-ordination of group plans. The representative group provides a manageable and interesting way for all groups to make their work public.

The representative group consists of a member from each of the groups in the class. Representatives may be assigned by the teacher or chosen by each group. The teacher often serves as chairperson but this position may also be held by a student.

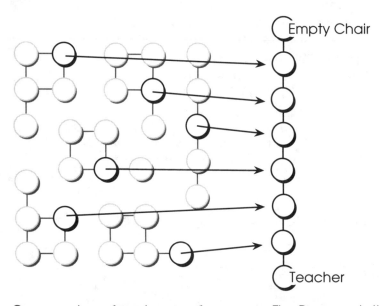

One member of each group forms ⟶ The Representative Group

The representative group may meet apart from the class. In this case, group members are responsible to report back to their groups on the work or decisions of the representative group. Alternatively, a "fishbowl" method may be used. The representative group sits in a circle around which the rest of the class sits to form an audience.

When the fishbowl method is used, one empty chair is included in the circle. Any class member may contribute to the discussion by sitting in that chair, but must give up the chair as soon as his/her point is made.

Initially, teachers may find the empty chair is used infrequently. However, as students become comfortable with this group structure, the empty chair adds a busy, lively, and exciting dimension to the discussion.

Representative groups can be used at any stage of the learning process. The purpose may be for informal progress reporting from groups or for longer discussion panels with well-prepared presentations from each group. Representative groups can be used in conjunction with any of the other kinds of groupings as one efficient way of obtaining information from each group working within the class.

Four Uses of Representative Groups

① Presenting

A representative group provides an efficient forum for group presentations to the whole class.

Sample Activities

Geography

The class is beginning a study of population patterns. All groups are given the same map and information about an unsettled region in a particular era. Groups are asked to predict population densities as the region is settled and provide a rationale for their predictions. Representatives from each group visit every other group in turn to present their group's prediction and rationale and to receive comments and questions. The teacher keeps track of time and informs the representatives when it is time to move to the next group. When all representatives complete the circuit, home groups hold a discussion to consider their predictions in the light of considerations from other groups' decisions.

Media Literacy

The class has discussed a societal issue and viewed a short documentary film. The teacher and students identify brief segments which have strong emotional impact related to the theme of the film. Each small group is assigned one of these segments to observe during a second viewing in order to analyze the director's techniques. Within each group, each student selects a specific focus to observe, for example, the lighting, camera angle, type of shot, and music. A representative from each group forms a panel. The representatives report the findings of their groups. The teacher chairs a panel discussion to explore how the director created the shots in the film to influence the audience. The empty chair is used to invite participation from the rest of the class.

Technological Studies

Each group has completed a different project. Projects are displayed at the various group work stations. Each group leaves one member at its work station to present and answer questions about its project. The other members of each group visit each station in turn.

Co-ordinating

② Steering committees can be helpful in co-ordinating class projects which involve a number of groups.

Sample Activities

Outdoor Education
The class is producing a news journal to report on a four-day excursion to an Outdoor Education School. Each group has responsibility for a different section — front page, people, ecology, wildlife, food, humour, and entertainment. A steering committee composed of one representative from each group meets with the teacher briefly during each work period to co-ordinate the layout, graphics, time lines, and sharing of resources.

Physical Education
A grade eight class is organizing a co-operative playday for the school. The class has identified major organizational tasks and has formed groups responsible for each task. A steering committee consisting of one member from each group co-ordinates the project and provides a forum for problem solving. This committee also creates a list of criteria for evaluating the day, designs an evaluation form for all students and teachers, and meets afterward to discuss evaluation results and to report back to the class.

Theme Study
Each small group is working on a subtopic related to a theme. The teacher holds a brief daily meeting with a co-ordinating committee composed of one representative from each group. The co-ordinating committee discusses the progress of the groups, organizes resources for the next steps, solves ongoing problems, and plans a culminating festival in which each group presents its work.

③ Problem Solving

Representative groups can provide a forum for solving problems such as the following ones:

- how to improve class behaviour in assemblies;
- how to get along with younger students in the school yard;
- how to set time lines for getting work done in groups;
- how to co-ordinate the efforts of group members;
- how to improve study skills.

The teacher might choose five students from the class to form a representative group. This group operates on behalf of the class and ultimately will present the results of its work to the class. If groups are already formed in the class the representative group is made up of one member from each of the other groups. Either the representative group can work on problems and report back to the groups or the groups brainstorm possible solutions which their representatives bring forward for discussion in the representative group meeting. Problem-solving meetings of this kind may be "fishbowled" by the rest of the class.

④ Peer Tutoring

The teacher can teach a skill or concept to members of the representative group. Students practise and help one another learn in the representative group before each member returns to his/her own group to teach the skill or concept. The teacher rotates the membership of the representative group so that, over time, every class member has a chance to participate.

Sample Peer Tutoring Activities

Computer Studies

The class is divided so that each group of four students shares the use of two computers. One representative from each group meets with the teacher to learn a new computer program and returns to teach and practise with the rest of his/her group.

Co-operative Skills

The representative group works with the teacher to learn how to chair a meeting successfully. Members then return to their own groups to explain the role of a chairperson and to model the role in a number of work periods.

Research Skills

The representative group goes to the library to work with the teacher-librarian to learn and practise a specific research skill. The representative members then return to the classroom to teach their groups and to bring their groups to the library to practise.

Visual Arts

Each group is designing a bulletin board or poster for the school. A representative group meets with the teacher for specialized instruction, for example, on lettering, composition, colour, and so on. The representatives return to their own groups to teach the other members.

Summary

This chapter has explored the five kinds of groups which are summarized in the chart below. It is likely that a teacher would use more than one kind of group during a unit of study and may use all five kinds of groupings throughout a term or semester to address a variety of learning objectives. As teachers become familiar and comfortable with the five kinds of groups they start to develop variations and combinations. The five ways provide the building blocks for expanded co-operative learning experiences. Ways of building expanded learning activities are described in Chapter Four.

Overview of the Five Kinds of Groups

Kind	Formation	Purposes	Uses
Informal	turn to those seated closest	to provide an immediate forum to talk through ideas	• guided practice • brainstorming • personal response • quick reports
Base	carefully formed by the teacher	to encourage peer support for learning	• coaching • collaborating
Combined	two or more groups join	to help each learn through consultation	• building information/expertise • analyzing information • reporting/presenting
Reconstituted	moving from a home group to a "cross" group and back to the home group	to gain a diversity of perspectives/insights	• exploring subtopics • exploring perspectives
Representative	a member from each group forms the representative	to provide a class forum for discussion	• presenting • co-ordinating • problem solving • peer tutoring

4 Building on the Five Kinds of Groups

What I want to learn most is all kinds of discussion techniques — to develop good discussion techniques, not only to use inside classes but also for when I'm out in the working force so I can get along better with my colleagues.

Rossana, Grade 9

In group work everyone has to contribute. I can't get bored or go to sleep. It's not as easy when we have a large class discussion, but I prefer it.

Mike, Grade 7

Successful co-operative learning activities are dependent upon an interplay of these five principles.

1. Students work in positive interdependence.

2. Students work in small heterogeneous groups.

3. Students are accountable both as individuals and as a group.

4. Students learn through ample opportunity for purposeful talk.

5. Students learn and practise co-operative skills as they study and explore the subject matter together.

These principles are introduced in Chapter One and included as part of discussion in Chapter Two. Chapters Three and Four demonstrate how the principles work in practical application. Chapters Five and Six provide information on the teaching of co-operative skills. Chapter Seven describes evaluation methods.

As the students work in small groups, it is satisfying to watch their ability to work together grow, and to see respect for their classmates increase.

Elementary Teacher

Nineteen countries and many age groups are represented in my class. Co-operative learning is ideal for fostering language development and social skills at the same time. The talking comes more naturally because the students get to know each other and talk about topics of shared interest.

Secondary Teacher

Co-operative learning creates a miniature community. Students can learn the skills we all need for life in larger communities.

Elementary Teacher

Building on the Five Kinds of Groups

This chapter demonstrates how the five kinds of groups described in Chapter Three can be used to build expanded learning activities. This chapter introduces three ways of building such activities.

1. Repeating the Grouping

Any of the five kinds of groups can be repeated during a learning experience. For example, informal groups can be repeated frequently during a unit of study. Similarly, reconstituted groups, such as Jigsaw, can be used at the beginning of a unit to access a broad base of information and at the conclusion to review and consolidate.

2. Extending the Grouping

Any of the five kinds of groups can be extended over a longer period. Base groups used over the course of an entire year are an obvious example. Informal groups can work for an entire period on an engaging topic. Representative groups can be used throughout an entire unit of study for peer tutoring.

3. Linking Two or More Groupings

Two or more of the five kinds of groups can be linked together to enhance interaction and facilitate deeper exploration of the topic. For example, two base groups can meet together as combined groups to consult. Informal groups can be set up spontaneously in the middle of a Jigsaw to solve a class difficulty.

The three ways provide teachers with a framework to develop and understand expanded learning activities. Through variation, teachers can even develop activities which link groupings and, at the same time, repeat and extend them. There are an infinite number of possibilities. This chapter develops one example of each of the three ways of building expanded activities and then describes Group Investigation, a formal method which effectively amalgamates all three ways.

Expanded learning activities are more successful in classrooms where students and teachers have experience working in groups and applying co-operative skills. For this reason the information in this chapter may be more relevant and useful to teachers after they have been using the ideas in Chapters Three and Five for some time.

One Example of Repeating the Grouping: Snowballing

Snowballing repeats combined groups so that groups expand in size from pairs, to fours, to eights, even to the whole class. The use of combined groups is described in detail in Chapter Three. Repeating combined groups encourages students to compose, amalgamate, expand, and orally synthesize ideas. Students have the security of peer support for learning as they continuously reshape information and concepts.

Snowballing can be a flexible and energizing learning experience which is completed in a single class period. It can also be used as one additional technique to facilitate learning at a particular stage of a larger unit of study. The following example, of an intermediate-level English class, demonstrates how snowballing can be carried out in one class period.

Students read a poem in pairs. Individually, each partner writes a few questions which come to mind about the poem. Then, together they select or revise three questions from the original lists.

Two pairs combine and try to answer the other pair's questions. Then as a group of four, they choose three questions that most interest them and have not been answered.

Two groups of four combine and once more try to answer each the other group's questions. They formulate three new or related questions that intrigue the group of eight. This time, however, a member from each group of eight writes the questions on the chalkboard.

Each group selects a second member to explain to the whole class why the three questions are interesting and important to the group. The teacher identifies the questions which are common to two or more groups and chairs a class discussion on each. Together the class works to synthesize contradictions of interpretation.

By the end of this experience students have discussed and personalized many perspectives of the poem. Students return to the original pair and individually write their personal responses to the poem in consultation with their partner.

One Example of Extending the Grouping: Extended Jigsaw

Jigsaw can be extended to provide a framework for major projects or units of study. Jigsaw uses reconstituted groups which are described in detail in Chapter Three. The following example of an intermediate-level Social Geography unit demonstrates the use of Extended Jigsaw.

Step 1: Introduction

The teacher chairs class discussion on the advantages and disadvantages of owning imported and domestic cars. The class forms home groups. Each group is assigned a section of the school parking lot. Each group is asked to identify the make and country of origin of each automobile in its section. This information is collated on a large chart on the classroom wall so that patterns can be analyzed. Each home group is given a specific task, such as finding out the proportion of cars from each country outside North America and the proportion of cars from each of the three major North American manufacturers. One purpose of this introductory stage is to help students develop an experimental interest in the project.

Next, each home group member is assigned a role related to a hypothetical domestic car manufacturing plant. The roles are manager, advertising executive, labour leader, and town council member. Each group is asked to imagine that the manufacturing plant is running into difficulties in part because of successful foreign competition. What can be done?

Step 2: Exploration

Students meet in exploration groups by role. All the managers meet in one group; all the advertising executives in another, and so on. Each exploration group examines the situation from the perspective of the group role. Each group is given an information sheet about the role. Each examines news media reports and does its own research in the resource centre. From its own role perspective each group drafts a plan of action to save the plant.

Step 3: Reporting/Reshaping

Students return to their home groups and discuss in role how best to save the plant. In this reshaping phase, the conversations among managers, labour leaders, advertising executives, and town councillors become quite animated. Each home group works to develop a mutually agreeable plan of action or to understand why members can't agree.

Step 4: Integration/Evaluation

Each home group prepares a presentation to give to the rest of the class. Groups use a wide variety of formats and materials, including maps, diagrams, debates, role plays, and displays.

Following each presentation each of the other groups meets to complete a response sheet of comments for the presenting group. The comments include what each group likes and the concerns or wishes each group has about the presentation. In addition to this peer evaluation each group receives a grade and comments from the teacher.

To personalize understanding, each student writes a short essay describing the highlights of the experience, what he/she learned from someone else's presentation, and what he/she learned about how to work with other people.

One Example of Linking Two or More Groupings: Interdependent Learning

Linking two or more of the five kinds of groups provides opportunities for increased interaction and facilitates deeper exploration of a topic. The following example illustrates how all five kinds of groups can be linked to enrich and make more effective what might otherwise be treated as a traditional independent learning project. The interdependent learning which results encourages students to develop and apply independant inquiry skills, which include viewing themselves and others as mutually supportive learning resources.

The teacher introduces a topic to the class and provides some initial exploration activities so that each student can identify areas of interest for individual inquiry. As described below, the five kinds of groups are linked to enrich individual learning during a four-week unit of study. Detailed descriptions of the five kinds of groups are found in Chapter Three.

Base Groups

The students are already organized in base groups for the semester. The teacher asks the base groups to meet formally once a week to provide ongoing research support — identifying difficulties and helping group members find solutions. The teacher provides agendas and time lines for the base group meetings. Base groups arrange extra time to work together and make group requests for library assistance.

Reconstituted Groups

To provide a base of information, the teacher collects articles related to the topic. She uses a Jigsaw activity to explore the articles. Each member of a base group selects one article to explore and meets with three other people interested in studying that source. Upon returning to their base groups, members report on their learning. The teacher shows a film which helps to consolidate the information.

Informal Groups

Throughout presentations, before and after films, and during brainstorming sessions, students meet in informal groups to discuss responses, generate ideas, and develop questions. On these occasions, students turn to another person close by. The composition of the groups varies throughout the four weeks.

Combined Groups

Twice during the four weeks, the teacher asks each base group to meet with another base group on a consultative basis. Each base group identifies two problems raised by the process of independant inquiry and lists strategies it has used or is thinking of using to address those problems. The two base groups combine to share ideas and help one another.

Representative Groups

One member of each base group acts as a representative of the group and joins a representative group meeting once a week to report to the teacher on the progress of the group members. These sessions afford the teacher opportunities to communicate with all groups via the representative. As well, the teacher uses this opportunity to teach organizational skills to the group representatives who then return to teach their base groups. The representative group discusses common problems and shares resources.

Amalgamating the Three Ways of Building Expanded Activities: Group Investigation

Group Investigation is one example of a formal method of using groups to facilitate in-depth study. It amalgamates the three ways of building expanded learning activities which have been discussed in this chapter. It repeats the use of informal groups, extends the use of representative groups, and links these two with the use of base groups. These three kinds of groups are described in detail in Chapter Three.

Group Investigation promotes self-directed learning. It provides opportunity for individual, small group, and whole class work. The class is organized into groups which investigate subtopics of a general class topic for an extended period. The groups provide support, encouragement, and resources for members. A steering committee formed of one representative from each group helps to plan and co-ordinate the overall class study.

In general, Group Investigation involves the following six steps.

Group Investigation

1. Identifying Subtopics and Forming Groups

2. Planning the Investigation

3. Carrying Out the Investigation

4. Preparing the Report

5. Presenting the Report

6. Evaluation

Group Investigation was developed by Yael Sharan, Shlomo Sharan and Rachel Hertz-Lazarowitz. A description of this approach can be found in: R. Slavin et al. (eds.), *Learning to Co-operate, Co-operating to Learn* (New York: Plenum Press, 1985).

The following example describes the experience of one secondary-level English class investigating Utopian literature in a six-week unit of study.

Step 1: Identifying Subtopics and Forming Groups
In preparation, students read two of the following novels: *We, Brave New World,* and *Walden*. They kept notes in their response journals for each book. These journals were shared with the teacher and became the basis for stimulating further inquiry.

Next, each student wrote a short essay in which he/she identified a societal problem and suggested a Utopian solution. The next day the essays were read and discussed in informal groups. One essay from each group was presented to the class by someone other than the author of the essay. The class discussed the meaning of Utopia, why the topic has fascinated people throughout history, and why it is so difficult to come to a concensus on what is Utopian.

The next day students individually wrote for five minutes identifying intriguing problems or topics on Utopias. Then informal groups of four or five consolidated their lists to present to the whole class. The teacher asked for one topic from each group and continued this process until all ideas were written on the chalkboard. Then the teacher asked the class to categorize the topics into major areas.

The major areas were categorized as follows: philosophy and religion; science and technology; education and child care; government and politics; personal and family relationships. Students were asked to form interest groups, each of which were to investigate one area.

In order to keep the groups both heterogeneous and similar in size a few students were asked to volunteer to move to another group. In one case eight students wished to work on the same topic. To keep groups small, that group divided into two smaller groups of four, each investigating the same topic.

Step 2: Planning the Investigation
Now that students had decided on a general topic and had formed groups they were ready to begin to plan their investigation by addressing the following questions.

- What will we focus on within our area of interest?
- Individually and as a group, what do we wish to learn?
- How will we organize our study?
- Where will we try to obtain information?
- What will we do with it?
- How will we divide up the responsibilities?
- What thesis might each of us develop in our individual essays?
- What kind of presentation might we make to the class?
- How will we periodically evaluate our effectiveness as a group and make changes in our operation to improve our effectiveness?

At this point the steering committee met for the first time. Its tasks over the next few weeks were as follows:

Compare notes on what each group is doing to check:

- that there is no unneccessary duplication;
- if there are any interesting connections among the group projects;
- if groups can assist each other in generating ideas and finding materials or sharing certain tasks.

Make decisions regarding the presentations:

- Decide on what dates and in what order the group presentations will be;
- Decide if the presentations will be completely separate from each other or if they will be connected in some way.

In consultation with the teacher, prepare evaluation activities.

During the first meeting the steering committee addressed only the first task. At the end of each meeting the teacher received a short informal report of what had been discussed and decided.

Each group recorded tentative plans on a progress report sheet provided by the teacher. The group representative brought this progress report to the steering committee for information purposes. Progress reports were filled out a number of times during the project. Each group's reports were filed in a separate folder. The teacher visited each group several times and reviewed the progress reports with the groups.

Step 3: Carrying Out the Investigation
The groups investigated their chosen topics. Although individually responsible for gathering information, analyzing data, and reaching tentative conclusions, students also assisted one another in their investigative group as they exchanged, discussed, clarified, and synthesized ideas. The steering committee continually relayed information and planning ideas between itself, the teacher, and the various groups.

The teacher distributed a short bibliography of both classic and contemporary Utopian writings. Students read and collected data for the individual essays over a two-week period. They were encouraged to assist each other in their research and to use the teacher as a resource. Each student selected one or two members of his/her group as peer editors. Thus students were ultimately responsible for their own essays and also assisted others.

Step 4: Preparing the Report
Because students were working and consulting together ideas flowed freely both within and among groups. The steering committee suggested a unified class presentation. The class would create its own version of *Walden* and ask the teacher to take the role of the visiting professor. The visitor would "tour" the imaginary Walden community. The "tour" would consist of a skit or demonstration related to the topic chosen by each group.

Planning for the final report involved an interplay of planning between the class as a whole and the class as separate groups. Students frequently met outside in the hall or in various corners of the school for rehearsal.

Step 5: Presenting the Report
The "tour" took three 60 minute periods. Each skit had a common format — what the world used to be like in the 1980's and what it is in the imaginary Utopian present. Between skits, about ten minutes were required to rearrange the classroom furniture, put on simple costumes, and set up props. After each skit the reasoning behind the presentation was explained and a question-and-answer dialogue completed the visit. The presentations were variously moving, challenging, humourous, and intellectually stimulating. After the presentations were concluded the teacher chaired a class discussion on how the experience had affected students. Highlights and insights were shared.

Step 6: Evaluation
Students participated in the following evaluation activities which had been worked out by the steering committee and the teacher early in the project. Peer, self, and teacher evaluation were all included.

- Students handed in their individual essays to the teacher for marking.
- Each group completed an anecdotal evaluation for every other group's presentation using criteria decided upon by the steering committee.
- The teacher evaluated each group's presentation using the same criteria.
- Each group reviewed the progress reports that had been on file during the project, discussed ways in which the group was effective in working together, and considered how to increase the group's effectiveness next time.
- Several weeks later a test involving a passage from *Walden* was given to the class. The insights and subtleties in the students' answers on the test were ample proof that sustained and integrated learning had taken place.

Further Suggestions for Group Investigation

The example above illustrates an intense six-week study at a senior level. Group Investigation has many other applications and may be well used by younger students. Like other co-operative learning methods it is flexible and can be used to organize school projects and to explore topics in many subject areas.

School Projects

Group investigation is a useful approach to school projects. Large projects can be divided into subtasks around which to form groups. The steering committee co-ordinates the subtasks throughout the project. Following is a list of examples of such projects:

- running a student council;
- planning a school event such as a concert, an open house, a dance, a festival, a career day, a co-operative playday;
- organizing a class/school excursion;
- developing a school code of behaviour with students, parents, and teachers;
- organizing a class play;
- facilitating a parent/teacher association activity.

Subject Study

Group Investigation is useful for exploring topics in many subject areas. Topics can be divided into subtopics around which to form groups. Following is a list of examples of such studies.

Science Fair Projects
The class selects a theme, such as ecology, space travel, or inventions, to focus its problem-solving activities. Interest areas are identified and groups are formed. The six steps of group investigation serve as an organizational plan for the development of co-operative science fair projects. The steering committee channels information and plans among the groups, co-ordinates the presentation plans, and provides criteria for ongoing evaluation throughout the project.

Social and Environmental Studies: Pioneer Study
The class has completed a unit of study on pioneer life. Students form interest groups based on different areas of pioneer life: food, social activity, education, family life, work life, and so on. The groups create projects such as making filmstrips, murals, booklets, or presenting plays to further extend their understanding. The steering committee co-ordinates plans and presentations.

Technological Studies: Woodworking
All students in the class have learned basic techniques on specific equipment: band saw, lathe, jointer, drill, and chisels. Students form interest groups to experiment and solve design problems to produce a finished product. The steering committee meets with the teacher to problem solve, make progress reports, and design the presentation format.

Work Experience
During the orientation period, before beginning their work experience in the community, students form interest groups to research subtopics on a theme such as "Effective Interpersonal Relations." The steering committee keeps the teacher informed on progress, solves problems and co-ordinates group presentations.

Summary

In summary, this chapter has introduced three ways of building expanded learning activities — repeating the grouping, extending the grouping, and linking two or more of the groupings. Additionally, this chapter has provided an illustration of Group Investigation — one formal method that amalgamates the three ways of building expanded activities.

Expanded activities provide students with opportunities for deeper involvement in the process of learning. Students apply their thinking skills by posing their own questions, defining a purpose for collecting information, organizing and synthesizing ideas, communicating their findings to others, and reflecting on their learning experiences.

Students work interdependently. The whole class meets to receive information or instruction from the teacher, to discuss common problems, or to communicate group findings. Students meet in small groups to pursue shared interests, to plan their work, and to support and enrich one another's learning. Students work individually to investigate subtopics or subthemes related to their small group interests.

Students are engaged in a variety of learning experiences, a number of which are self-selected as well as collaboratively designed in the small groups. The balance between self-direction, group autonomy, and teacher guidance will depend upon the needs of students and teachers.

Expanded learning activities are more successful in classrooms where students and teachers have experience working in groups and applying co-operative skills. Information on teaching co-operative skills is provided in Chapter Five.

5 Teaching Co-operative Skills

In group work you get to know people as individuals. You get to know how they feel and what they think.

Danny, Grade 7

Successful co-operative learning activities are dependent upon an interplay of these five principles.

1. Students work in positive interdependence.

2. Students work in small heterogeneous groups.

3. Students are accountable both as individuals and as a group.

4. Students learn through ample opportunity for purposeful talk.

5. Students learn and practise co-operative skills as they study and explore the subject matter together.

These principles are introduced in Chapter One and included as part of discussion in Chapter Two. Chapters Three and Four demonstrate how the principles work in practical application. Chapters Five and Six provide information on the teaching of co-operative skills. Chapter Seven describes evaluation methods.

I like to be an observer. I can ask questions to learn about what the students are thinking. The students feel proud when they teach the teacher by talking about their ideas.

Elementary Teacher

I've come to appreciate the role of facilitator. I was nervous at first, but now I see that people learn more when I'm less in charge. I realize it's better if I don't do all the thinking and talking.

Secondary Teacher

By watching the students working together in small groups I become aware of the strengths of each of the students.

Elementary Teacher

Teaching Co-operative Skills

This chapter provides suggestions for helping students to learn co-operative skills. Initially, teachers may want to read the chapter to get an overview of the process and the strategies which could be used. It is not intended that each teacher employ all of the strategies. Needs will vary from one classroom to another. Teachers can introduce skills which are most pertinent to the needs of their students and choose strategies with which they feel comfortable. Teachers can return to this chapter for more ideas as new needs become apparent.

The objectives for teaching co-operative skills are the following:

- to foster a climate of trust and respect in which students feel it is safe to take the risk of learning and practise new skills;
- to enable each student to feel valued as a member of a group;
- to facilitate productive academic learning through successful group interaction.

It is important to teach students the co-operative skills required for working together. Many students are accustomed to working individually to learn. They are also accustomed to close supervision of their work and behaviour by the teacher. They may be unfamiliar with the autonomy, collaboration, and mutual responsibility involved in group learning. Moreover, in groups, students will likely be working with classmates who differ from themselves in skills and background. In order for co-operative group work to be productive and satisfying, students will need guidance in developing co-operative skills.

Examples of Co-operative Skills

There are two kinds of co-operative skills. Task skills are those which group members use to complete the academic work. Working relationship skills are those which help build and sustain the group's disposition and ability to work together. Following are examples of the two kinds of co-operative skills.

① Task Skills

- Asking Questions
- Asking for Clarification
- Checking for Others' Understanding
- Elaborating on Others' Ideas
- Following Directions
- Getting the Group Back to Work
- Keeping Track of Time
- Listening Actively
- Sharing Information and Ideas
- Staying on Task
- Summarizing for Understanding/Paraphrasing

② Working Relationship Skills

- Acknowledging Contributions
- Checking for Agreement
- Disagreeing in an Agreeable Way
- Encouraging Others
- Expressing Support
- Inviting Others to Talk
- Keeping Things Calm/Reducing Tension
- Mediating
- Responding to Ideas
- Sharing Feelings
- Showing Appreciation

The Process of Learning Co-operative Skills

The natural process by which people learn also describes how students learn to work more effectively with others. Becoming aware of this learning cycle and incorporating it into classroom activity greatly enhances the teaching and learning of co-operative skills.

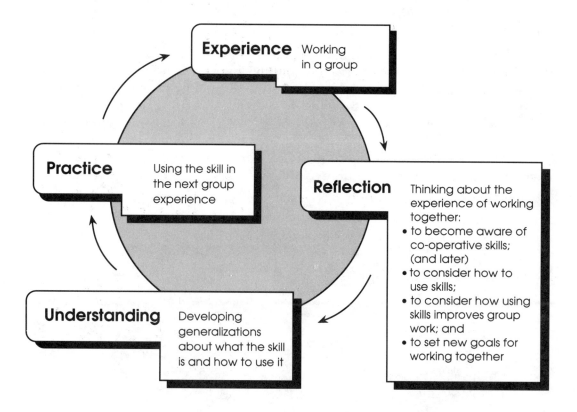

Experience Working in a group

Reflection Thinking about the experience of working together:
- to become aware of co-operative skills; (and later)
- to consider how to use skills;
- to consider how using skills improves group work; and
- to set new goals for working together

Understanding Developing generalizations about what the skill is and how to use it

Practice Using the skill in the next group experience

With the teacher's guidance students develop co-operative skills gradually through repeated opportunities to work together, to reflect, to understand, and to practise co-operative skills.

On the following pages, strategies for addressing each stage of the learning cycle are described. In each stage, teachers can select or create activities which will be most helpful for their students.

Providing Students with Experience in Small Group Work

Learning co-operative skills begins with the experience of working together. As groups work, the teacher is able to observe and begin to identify the co-operative skills which students use well and those skills which need emphasis. This information helps the teacher to guide students in reflecting on their experience.

Focusing on the Academic Task

In most cases teachers will use academic subject matter as the focus for initial group activities. There are many suggestions in Chapters Two and Three for short, simple academic activities which introduce students to the experience of working in groups. Even if students are experienced with group work, teachers may still begin with short, simple, academic group tasks that provide a comfortable way for students to meet and work with many people in the class. Novel academic activities which arouse students' curiosity are particularly useful. So are open-ended activities which encourage diverse responses rather than right and wrong answers.

Focusing on Working Together

In classrooms where there is social tension or competitiveness it may be helpful to minimize academic demands in initial experiences of working together. There are a number of suggestions for non-academic activities in Chapter Two. There are also many non-academic activities in sources such as Spencer Kagan's *Co-operative Learning Resources for Teachers* (University of California: School of Education, 1985) and Dee Dishon and Chick Moorman's *Our Classroom — We Can Learn Together* (Englewood Cliffs: Prentice-Hall, 1983). Instead of emphasizing an academic task, such initial activities focus directly on helping students know one another. They build positive working relationships, and demonstrate that co-operation can be satisfying. They set the stage for successful academic activity later on.

Helping Students Reflect on Their Experience

After the initial group learning experience the teacher can help students to reflect on that experience, through a combination of class discussion, group discussion, and individual reflection. Discussion topics such as the following encourage a growing awareness of the need to learn co-operative skills. Students can be encouraged to identify a few skills they use effectively and a few they could learn to use more effectively.

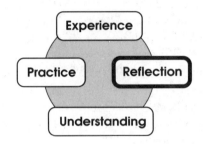

Reflecting on the Need to Learn Co-operative Skills

- The class can brainstorm to identify skills necessary for co-operative group work.
- The class can brainstorm a list of guidelines for effective group work.
- Groups can consider what contributed to effective group functioning.
- Groups can consider what got in the way of effective group functioning.
- Groups can consider what members might do differently next time.
- Groups can identify links between the use of co-operative skills and how successful the group was in completing the academic task.
- Individual students can consider how they contributed to their group's effective functioning.
- Individual students can consider what they did which caused problems in their groups.
- Individual students can consider what they might do the same/differently next time.

Understanding Skills

Once students have become aware of the need to learn skills and have identified some skills they need to learn, the teacher can teach these skills. Skills, such as forming groups quietly, sharing a work space, sharing information and ideas, and encouraging others, are often identified first by students. Later, students identify more complex skills such as clarifying, paraphrasing, or synthesizing different ideas into an integrated perspective.

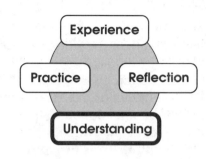

Often students don't have a repertoire of the language and behaviour that puts co-operation into practice. Empowering students to interact effectively involves giving them access to such a repertoire. One way of teaching a skill, therefore, is to ask students to brainstorm what the skill sounds like and looks like when it is practised.

The chart below is the kind of list a class might make about the skill of "Sharing Information and Ideas." Such charts can be posted on the classroom wall for reference, further discussion, and expansion.

Sharing Information and Ideas

Sounds Like	*Looks Like*
• *What do you think?*	Smile
• *My guess is that...*	Nod
• *Let's look back to...*	Eye contact
• *I understand; you are explaining...*	Head nodding
• *Another idea might be...*	Leaning forward
• *I think...*	Head tilted to side

Once students have begun to understand a skill, they could develop simple observation forms based on their lists to collect information about the use of that skill in their group. It is helpful to encourage them to share anecdotal examples of how they, or another group member, used the skill effectively. This helps both the student telling the story and other students to develop greater understanding.

Another strategy is to focus on particular language or behaviours that can hinder group interaction. The teacher might observe these situations during group work and present analogous hypothetical situations for consideration by the class. For example, in one situation a student, seeking clarification of one group member's contribution, turns to another group member and says "What did he say?" The teacher asks students to brainstorm ways of seeking clarification which are more effective, inclusive, and sensitive to another's feelings. The chart below is an example of the kind of lists students might make.

Alternatives to "What Did He Say?"

- *I'm sorry, I didn't get that. Would you repeat it, please?*
- *I missed that.*
- *Would you run that by me again?*
- *Pardon me?*

No matter what other ways are used to teach skills, it is essential that teachers model their use during interactions with students. Teaching by example is very powerful because students learn far more from how adults behave than from how adults say students should behave. For example, when teachers say, "This didn't work too well today: how can we improve it?", they are modelling the sharing of leadership and asking for the opinions of others. When teachers say, "Jan, you looked like you wanted to say something...", they are demonstrating encouragement and awareness of others' feelings.

Providing Opportunities for Practice

At the beginning of a work period the teacher can ask the students to practise skills as they work on the academic task. Often students choose skills they have already identified and learned about. Occasionally, the teacher may assign a skill for all groups to practise. For example, there are some skills which every student needs to learn in order to make group work manageable within a classroom. Skills such as forming groups quietly, staying with the group, using a quiet voice, and organizing resources all contribute to the productive functioning of the class as a whole.

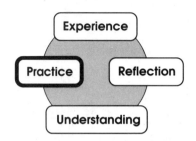

Practice provides experience for further reflective activity. The teacher can circulate among the groups to observe and make notes on skills being used and skills which are needed. Verbal reports by the teacher on his/her observations can guide future reflection. Setting group goals and practising together over time will enable students to see progress and develop a group sense of responsibility for, and satisfaction with, their interaction.

If groups need greater structure the teacher might assign a role to each group member. The roles might include, "encourager," "summarizer," "clarifier," "co-ordinator," and "recorder." Assignments can be rotated so each student is given an opportunity to practise each skill. Role-assignment cards such as the one below are helpful.

Co-ordinator

It is your responsibility over the course of this group project to co-ordinate the schedule of your group work. You will record the plans and target dates, remind your group of time lines, and check off each stage on the master class schedule.

Sometimes nonacademic group activities can be used for practice purposes. These activities have the additional benefit of fostering group cohesion when that is needed. Teachers sometimes find that during a period of demanding academic work, group communication skills may deteriorate. Nonacademic group activities can re-establish friendly interaction.

Activities such as those described in Chapter Two, which use light, humourous questions, are useful. So are many of the activities in sources such as the Spencer Kagan source noted on p. 93. Sometimes the activity of solving problems in logic is a useful way to demonstrate the effectiveness of co-operation. Such activities are found in sources such as *Quizzles* (W. Williams: Palo Alto, California: Dale Seymour Publications, 1976).

Physical activity can be a useful tension reliever for groups. The following activities also provide opportunity for practising skills and gaining experience for further reflection.

Sample Activities

Mirroring
In pairs, students stand facing each other. One partner makes hand or arm movements slowly enough for the other to mirror. Then the roles are reversed. The objective is for each pair to become so synchronized in its movements that an observer cannot tell who is the leader and who is the mirror image. This kind of activity can help students practise attentiveness to others and sensitive leading and following. The experience is helpful when it is related to the students' ways of interacting with other students during academic work. The appropriateness of the analogy should be discussed.

Trust Walk
In pairs, one student closes his/her eyes and the other leads him/her by the hand around the classroom. Then the roles are reversed. This kind of activity can provide practice in trusting and being trusted. The experience is helpful when it is related to the students' experience in working in groups. The appropriateness of the analogy should be discussed.

Repeating the Process

Students learn co-operative skills through repeated cycles of experience, reflection, understanding, and practice. Through reflecting on their own experience students discover the need to improve some aspect of their group's functioning or their own functioning within the group. They learn about the causes of difficulties in groups. They create and try out their own solutions. They experience the satisfaction of learning a new skill or overcoming a difficulty.

By paying explicit attention to the learning cycle and devoting class time to it the teacher is providing the message that working effectively in groups is important. Students shape their own learning and develop social confidence. Over time the cycles become spirals of increasing group effectiveness and academic learning.

Reflection is a key element in the learning cycle. It is the means by which students develop understanding of their experience. It is therefore important to provide regular opportunities, following group work, for students to reflect on the experience of working together and the ways co-operative skills can be employed to increase group effectiveness.

Questions and activities such as the ones on the following page and earlier in this chapter under the heading "Helping Students Reflect on Their Experience" can be used regularly. The forms at the end of this chapter provide simple ways of asking similar questions. Consistent use of the same questions or forms can help students chart their own development.

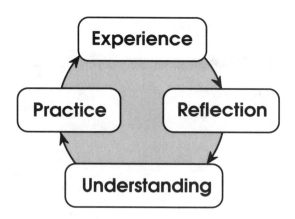

Activities Which Help Students Reflect

- Groups can be encouraged to make their own questions for reflection.

- Groups can write letters to the teacher at different stages to describe the growth and development of their group. This activity helps the group to define its personality and gives the teacher a window into the dynamics of the group.

- Students can take turns placing themselves outside the group and silently observing the interaction.

- Groups can record a work session on video tape and replay parts of it.

- Group members can report on an action they remember that demonstrated the use of a co-operative skill.

- The teacher can report on his/her own observation of the group. Saying "I noticed when you were talking about...you were all leaning forward toward one another.... I wondered what that meant" helps students reflect on the meaning behind behaviour. Saying "I heard some good ideas from some people in your group today.... How could you help everyone feel comfortable about participating?" helps students reflect on how they can improve group interaction.

One Teacher's Experience

The following illustration demonstrates how the learning cycle operates.

> One teacher found that her students initially experienced confusion about how to work effectively in groups. During the first group work period, not all group members felt accountable, felt responsible, or worked productively on the academic task. Some class members were perceived by their peers to be less able and were ignored or rejected as a result. Some class members were perceived to dominate the group and to restrict the contributions of others.
>
> The teacher waited through the difficulties of the first lesson because she wished to build student awareness of the need to learn co-operative skills. She started the next period by asking the class to brainstorm a list of skills which contribute to effective group functioning. The resulting list was organized under three headings — *discussion skills*, such as asking questions, clarifying meaning, and contributing ideas; *staying-on-task skills*, such as checking that everyone understands, and reminding others of the topic under discussion; and *leadership skills*, such as accepting opinions, encouraging others, and inviting others to contribute. Each group then selected a few skills which its members felt would help the group function more effectively and pleasantly. Next, each group created an observation form and appointed a different observer daily to keep track of the practice of these skills.
>
> At the end of each work session the observer reported to the group. Group members discussed how effectively they worked together. They identified two areas of strength and one area to work on in the next session. Typically, student conversation during this exercise included happy agreement with what the group did well — "We did it! Today we stayed right on task." As well, the discussions generally included astute comments on how the group could improve — "We really need to make sure everyone is listening. Sometimes a person was talking to just one person and not to the whole group. That doesn't help when we want everyone to contribute."

The illustration above demonstrates the importance of beginning with the experience of students. The teacher helped students to reflect on their experience working together. They came to some initial understanding of the skills that help groups operate effectively. Then the teacher provided opportunity for practice and the learning cycle was repeated. The observers' comments stimulated further reflection, goal setting, and understanding after each subsequent round of group activity.

Summary

In this chapter we have described the process by which students learn co-operative skills. New learning may be initially slow, followed by rapid improvement, then a period where performance remains the same, followed by another phase of improvement.

It is important to treat difficulties with understanding, reassurance, opportunity to reflect, and encouragement to try again. Difficulties can then motivate a desire to learn rather than generate discouragement or frustration.

At times it may be necessary to put the academic task aside temporarily in order to address needs for co-operative skills. Discussing students' feelings may help students and teacher to develop understanding of a problem. Encouraging groups to propose and try their own solutions may require a little time. It may be important at times to rebuild group cohesion through activities which are not demanding academically.

While it may seem like "losing time" to play down academic objectives in order to address social skills, academic productivity will be gained in the long run. Student motivation to learn will be enhanced by strengthening the collaborative interaction among students.

The process of developing co-operative skills may also enhance students' problem solving in academic tasks. Intellectual and social problems require the same thinking skills — the ability to identify problems, to propose and apply solutions, and to reflect on outcomes. Interaction with peers is a valuable way to learn these problem-solving strategies. Whereas academic problems are often hypothetical to students, group interaction provides "real" problems which students can think about and solve with each other.

The long-range goals of teaching co-operative skills are to help students enjoy working together, to care about each other's learning, and to produce a high standard of work. Steady attention to the process of experience, reflection, understanding, and practice will lead toward these long-range goals.

Individual Self-Evaluation Form

Students circle the face which best represents their feelings about how the members in the group worked together.

I listened to others in my group.

I shared ideas and information.

Others in my group listened to me.

Adapted from: The Board of Education for the City of Scarborough, *Co-operative Learning - The Jigsaw Strategy*, 1985:25.

Individual Self-Evaluation Form

Please fill in the number of squares which best represents your participation in the group work.

I encouraged others.

I shared my materials with others.

I checked to make sure others understood the work.

I was willing to give and receive help.

I accepted responsibility for completing the work properly.

Comments/Suggestions

_____

_____

_____

_____

_____

_____

_____

_____   _____
Signature   Date

Individual Group Evaluation Form

We will stop once weekly to hold discussion in your groups about the process of working together. This is a time to consider how you feel and what you think about working in your group. Thinking about the process of working together helps people to recognize strengths and to become aware of ways in which we can improve our working relationships.

Please answer the following three questions on your own. Then use the three questions and your response as the basis for discussion within your group.

1. How do you feel about your participation as a member of your group at this time?

Please circle:

Very Satisfied   **Quite Satisfied**   **Somewhat Dissatisfied**   **Quite Dissatisfied**

Please comment on why you checked where you did.

_____

_____

_____

2. How do you feel about the productivity of your group at this time?

Please circle:

Very Satisfied   **Quite Satisfied**   **Somewhat Dissatisfied**   **Quite Dissatisfied**

Please comment on why you checked where you did.

_____

_____

_____

3. What things might I, or we, do to improve our group functioning as we continue to work?

_____

_____

_____

Group Evaluation Form

Please fill out this form together. Ask one group member to chair the discussion.

1. Circle one

Our group	did not get started	got started pretty soon	got started immediately
Our group	did not stay on the topic	stayed on the topic to some extent	stayed on the topic well
Our group	did not co-operate	worked together to some extent	worked together quite well

2. Circle one

Everyone in our group contributed ideas.	Yes	No
Everyone on our group listened carefully to each other.	Yes	No
Everyone in our group tried to help others contribute thoughts and feelings.	Yes	No

3. One thing to do differently next time:

_____

_____

_____

_____

_____

_____

Group Evaluation Form

Please fill out this form together.

1. We check to make sure we understand directions.

      Always —————|————— **Never**

2. We share our materials and remember to take turns.

      Always —————|————— **Never**

3. We help one another.

      Always —————|————— **Never**

4. We praise one another.

      Always —————|————— **Never**

5. We listen without interrupting.

      Always —————|————— **Never**

Signatures: _____   Date: _____

_____

_____

_____

_____

Adapted from: The Saskatchewan Department of Co-operation and Co-operative Development, *Working Together, Learning Together*, 1983:89.

Group Evaluation Form

Please fill out this form together.

We Liked:

_____

_____

_____

_____

_____

_____

_____

_____

_____

_____

We Wished:

_____

_____

_____

_____

_____

_____

_____

_____

_____

_____

Ideas For Next Time We Work in Co-operative Groups:

_____

_____

_____

_____

_____

_____

_____

Group: _____ Date: _____

Group Evaluation Form

Please meet with your group and use the checklist below as a basis for discussing how effectively your group is working. Complete the checklist. This form will be returned to your group at the beginning of the next work session.

Use this scale.   **Strongly agree** | 1 | 2 | 3 | 4 | 5 | **Strongly disagree**

Our group:

a) identified clear goals;

| 1 | 2 | 3 | 4 | 5 |

b) made progress toward the goals;

| 1 | 2 | 3 | 4 | 5 |

c) shared information and ideas;

| 1 | 2 | 3 | 4 | 5 |

d) made decisions based on the views of all;

| 1 | 2 | 3 | 4 | 5 |

e) listened well to each other;

| 1 | 2 | 3 | 4 | 5 |

f) encouraged each other to participate.

| 1 | 2 | 3 | 4 | 5 |

One way we might improve our work is by:

_____

_____

_____

_____

Group Members: _____ Date:_____

_____

_____

_____

Group Goal-Setting Form

Date: _____

Group: _____

Please fill in this form together. Ask one group member to chair the discussion. Hand the completed form in to your teacher. It will be returned to you during your next class period.

1. Three ways we can help one another in our co-operative group:

     a) _____

     b) _____

     c) _____

2. Three ways we can help other group members feel good about being in our group:

     a) _____

     b) _____

     c) _____

3. Three ways we can help our teacher make our co-operative groups work:

     a) _____

     b) _____

     c) _____

Signatures: (Chair)

_____

_____

_____

_____

Adapted from: The Saskatchewan Department of Co-operation and Co-operative Development, *Working Together, Learning Together*, 1983:93.

Co-operative Language Form

We identified "Keeping on Task" and "Offering Praise and Encouragement" as co-operative skills to help groups work well. Language helps us use these skills effectively. In the spaces below list some of the helpful things you can say when you think someone is going off topic or when you would like to praise or encourage someone.

When you think someone is going off topic:

Maybe we can talk about that later. Right now, let's discuss...

_____

_____

_____

_____

_____

When you want to praise or encourage someone:

You explained that really well.

_____

_____

_____

_____

_____

Co-operative Language Form

We identified "asking for clarification" as a communication skill which helps groups work well. In the spaces below list some of the helpful things you can say when you want someone to repeat what he/she has said or when you want someone to explain what he/she has said.

When you want someone to repeat:

I'm sorry, I missed that. What did you say?

_____

_____

_____

_____

_____

When you want someone to explain:

Would you mind explaining that idea?

_____

_____

_____

_____

_____

Two Key Elements of the Teacher's Role

What I learned in co-operative group work about how to interact with people — learning to respect their opinions — I can apply right now in my everyday life.

Eric, Grade 8

Successful co-operative learning activities are dependent upon an interplay of these five principles.

1. Students work in positive interdependence.

2. Students work in small heterogeneous groups.

3. Students are accountable both as individuals and as a group.

4. Students learn through ample opportunity for purposeful talk.

5. Students learn and practise co-operative skills as they study and explore the subject matter together.

These principles are introduced in Chapter One and included as part of discussion in Chapter Two. Chapters Three and Four demonstrate how the principles work in practical application. Chapters Five and Six provide information on the teaching of co-operative skills. Chapter Seven describes evaluation methods.

Small group learning gives the teacher a chance to step back and watch the students interact. You get to know what their problem-solving and social skills are. It's interesting to see how the groups develop and to see more students take leadership roles.

Teacher of Gifted Classes

In the old style, I was too busy doing all the talking to figure out if the students were learning anything. It wasn't until the exam that I found out what the students had learned, and for some that was too late. With co-operative learning I can step back and look at what is really happening rather than going on what I think is happening.

Secondary Teacher

Two Key Elements of the Teacher's Role

This chapter examines two key elements of the teacher's role — observation and supportive intervention. While other roles such as preparing materials and designing activities are important, observing and intervening are critical for determining student needs, planning appropriately, and facilitating learning. These two key elements contribute to effective evaluation. Evaluation is explored in Chapter Seven.

During large group instruction it is difficult for the teacher to find time for observation. Co-operative small group learning, on the other hand, provides ample opportunity for the teachers to observe, reflect, and intervene in supportive ways.

Observing Groups at Work

Observing groups at work is a direct means for the teacher to learn how groups are functioning, what students are learning, and where they need assistance. By watching student interaction, the teacher can learn about students' interests, feelings, ways of thinking, and academic skills. The teacher can use observation for the following purposes:

- to evaluate academic learning and identify where assistance is needed;
- to evaluate group interaction and identify where assistance is needed;
- to provide a basis for the teacher's own reflection regarding learning and teaching strategies;
- to provide a basis for supportive intervention.

Strategies for Observing

In the early stages of co-operative group work, students may need the teacher's assistance on a regular basis. As a result, there may be little time for systematic observation of all groups. When approaching a group that needs assistance, a few minutes of observation may enable the teacher to intervene supportively, for example, by making a comment or posing a question which will encourage students to consider possible solutions to their difficulty. As group work becomes easier for students, the teacher will have more time for circulating about the room, gathering information about several or all of the groups.

Observing is most useful when it is guided by a question which the teacher would like to answer. The following two observation methods may lead to insights and further questions. It is helpful to begin with the more informal method, "Global Observation," and to move toward "Systematic Observation" to test out hunches about what is going on.

Global Observation

Stand back to watch and listen to the groups at work. Record what you see and hear.

- Are the students huddled together over the task?
- Does anyone appear detached—leaning away from the group, attention wandering?
- Do you see gestures which may indicate interest, involvement, boredom, unhappiness, frustration?
- Record what you hear. What is the tone of group talk? Is it friendly, animated, argumentative? Can you tell if the students are working on the task?
- Reflect on what you saw and heard. What might be reasons why students were doing what you saw and heard?

Systematic Observation

Checklists help the teacher focus his/her observation. Teachers can prepare observation checklists by identifying essential skills for co-operative interaction and by choosing one or two co-operative skills to observe. The lists of skills which students generate from their experience working in groups are very useful for this purpose. The observation checklists included at the end of this chapter provide useful models.

Using Checklists Effectively

- Be unobtrusive as you observe. It is important not to take students' attention away from the work they are doing in their groups.
- Plan the observation. Decide how many groups you will observe and the length of time you will observe each group.
- Use one observation sheet for each group.
- Make a tally mark each time you observe the co-operative skill.
- Observe nonverbal communication such as facial expressions and body posture.
- Don't try to observe everything.
- Take a few minutes between groups to make notes on general impressions and important observations which do not fit into the categories on your observation sheet.
- Keep your observation sheets to assess growth over time. You could use one observation sheet per group per week and use a different coloured marker for each day's observation.

Observing for the Development of Thinking Skills

Observing groups at work is a valuable way to assess students' thinking skills. In individual work the teacher may have to infer students' thinking. In small group learning students' thinking skills are more explicitly evident because of the interactive, communicative nature of learning. One sign of productive learning during group discussion is hearing students apply various thinking skills such as posing questions, synthesizing ideas, and predicting outcomes.

The following questions could guide observation for thinking skills during small group learning. The teacher may choose to observe for signs of one or two thinking skills which are important in the current learning activity.

Observing for Thinking Skills

- Do the students pose questions?
  "I wonder if..." "It seems we don't know enough about..."
  "How are we going to...?"
- Do the students give reasons for their ideas?
  "I think... because..."
- Do the students use past knowledge and experiences?
  "This reminds me of..." "This is like when we did..."
- Do the students predict outcomes?
  "If we do..., then I think...will happen."
- Do the students see relationships among ideas?
  "...is like...because..." "...happened because..."
- Do the students consider other points of view by acknowledging or making reference to others' ideas, asking for elaboration, paraphrasing and synthesizing others' ideas?

Effective thinking and communication skills lead to productive group work. Teachers can help support the development of these skills.

> ### Encouraging Thinking Skills
>
> - Teachers can model questions that encourage thinking. "Why do you think...?" "What do you think might happen if...?" "Are there any similarities in what Quan and Mary are suggesting?"
> - Teachers can encourage students to give and to ask group members to explain the reasons for their ideas or opinions.
> - Teachers can encourage groups to explore the ideas presented before acting on them or rejecting them by considering the facts or values on which ideas are based, by considering evidence to support an idea, and by considering the application of an idea.
> - In the planning stages of a project teachers can encourage groups to focus more on posing questions about their topic and how they might proceed than on making quick decisions.

Facilitating effective thinking and communication in group work may reduce misunderstandings which can hamper group interaction, may enable the work to proceed in an organized manner, and may lead to a product that is satisfactory to all group members.

Concerns About Observation

Concern About What to Observe

It is important to observe systematically as well as globally. Observation checklists focus the observer's attention. It is helpful to remember that if an event or behaviour is important it will be repeated on other occasions.

Concern About Making Subjective Judgements

It is important to distinguish between observed behaviours and inferences about the meaning or effect of the behaviour on the group. For example, the teacher may observe a student sitting silently, not contributing to the group's discussion. Is the student listening and thinking about the discussion topic? Is the student distracted and not involved in the group work? These questions may provide a focus for further observation.

The teacher can verify inferences by sharing them with the group and seeking the students' opinions of the interpretation. For example, the teacher might say to a student, "I saw you sitting silently and wondered if you were thinking about the topic or if you were distracted."

Reflecting on Observations

Reflection enables the teacher to assess what has been observed. It provides the foundation for setting new goals for student learning and planning appropriate learning activities. The following strategies assist reflection.

- The teacher can reflect to identify possible explanations for what is observed. For example, problems can be identified tentatively and solutions considered. "I'm spending a lot of time keeping the groups on task lately. Am I encouraging this dependence by intervening too readily? Maybe I can try to find ways to help groups keep themselves on task."

- Teachers can "think out loud" with one or two colleagues. Describing thoughts out loud helps to make links between observations and interpretation. Questions and comments from a colleague may lead to a new perspective on student activity and on teaching practices.

- Teachers can make reflection notes on their completed observation sheets. Often notes take the form of impressions and questions. This is a way of recording thoughts for consideration at a future time. Notes made over time may reveal progress or a recurring difficulty which may not be evident on a day-to-day basis.

Intervening Supportively

Supportive intervention empowers students to work together more effectively. Often students perceive the teacher as judge and juror and want the teacher to solve their problems in getting along and in doing the academic work. Students will learn best, however, if the teacher usually resists the temptation to tell students what to do. With patience, encouragement, and opportunity to reflect, groups can often work through their own problems. The experience of working out their own solutions helps students learn skills for solving similar problems in the future.

The teacher can intervene to help groups solve their own problems in the following ways.

Acting as Facilitator

The most effective way a teacher can intervene is to facilitate students' problem solving.

- Teachers can encourage students to state their problem as a group problem rather than focussing on individual group members.
- Teachers can help students to state the problem using the sentence stem: "Our problem is how to..." If the students can state the problem in this way, they have taken the first step towards solving it.
- Teachers can encourage students to propose and then try possible solutions.

By acting as facilitator the teacher is telling students, "I have confidence in your ability to solve problems." Groups learn that problems are challenges they can address. With experience students will rely more and more on their own resources and feel less need to rely on the teacher's assistance.

so true!

Modelling

The teacher can intervene to model more constructive statements. A brief demonstration may help students understand what co-operative skills look and sound like.

Encouraging Group Discussion of Feelings

Recognizing and expressing feelings can be an important step in identifying and understanding problems. Students may need to express feelings before the group considers solutions to a problem. Recognition and expression of feelings is an important step in identifying problems. The teacher can facilitate a discussion of feelings and then encourage the group to consider what they can do, so members feel better about the group interaction.

Responding to Individual Difficulties

At times, individual students experience difficulties working co-operatively in a group. It is helpful to remember that all children want to be liked and accepted in the peer group. Occasionally a student may need individual assistance from the teacher. The main consideration for the teacher in finding a solution to problematic behaviour is to structure the student's role so that the student has an opportunity to learn a co-operative skill and feel like a valued member of a group. The following examples illustrate some ways in which teachers help students to participate successfully in a group.

The Student Who is Shy

- Using brief group activities can help to ease the student into group work.

- Using groups of three may be less demanding than pairs. Also, in a group of three, the shy student is less likely to be overlooked than in larger groups.

- Assigning the socially retiring student a role which he/she feels comfortable about taking in the group. The role may be that of reader, recorder, reporter, or observer. Through these roles, which demand less assertiveness, the student can make a valuable contribution to the group. In time, the student may develop the confidence to take a more active role in the group.

- Providing group tasks in which each member's contribution is specified helps to encourage participation; for example, in reconstituted groups each member learns specific information to contribute to the group. Other group members will actively involve the socially retiring student because each group member has information that the others need. Information on reconstituted groups is included in Chapter Three.

- Asking students to prepare their contributions ahead of time may help the retiring students feel more comfortable.

- Structuring the order of individual contributions in the group can reduce the possibility that a hesitant or reflective student will not have opportunity to speak. For example, teachers can ask students to number off to present ideas.

- Discussing co-operative skills with the anxious student before group work begins can help the student plan ways to feel at ease. Pre-discussion with periodic consultation to monitor the student's feelings and use of skills can increase the student's confidence.

The Student Who is Dominating

- Beginning with brief activities involving student exchange of ideas on individual work (rather than group activities which require a group product) may help equalize opportunities to participate. The student who wants to be individually successful may find it easier to develop the skills of listening and sharing when comments of others assist her/his individual learning.

- Assigning the role of observer, recorder, or reporter reduces the opportunity for a student to dominate group discussion while providing him/her the opportunity to make an important contribution to the group.

- Discussion with the student helps build awareness. If the student perceives that the teacher wants to understand and help, the student may be motivated to develop co-operative skills for effective group work. Together the student and teacher can identify a co-operative skill objective which the student is willing to work toward. This fosters student responsibility for behaviour and opens the door for the teacher to continue encouragement and support as the student experiments with the strategy.

The Student Who Dislikes Group Work

- Talking with the student to find out why he/she dislikes group work may help the teacher to understand the nature of the problem. Finding an appropriate solution will depend upon the nature of the problem. The following are two kinds of concerns students sometimes express.

The student dislikes group work because of lack of confidence that he/she will be accepted by others:

- Placing the student in a group with a classmate with whom he/she feels comfortable, or with students who will be supportive and accepting.

- Suggesting a role in which the student can use his/her particular talents.

The student is concerned about his/her individual grade (mark):

- Starting with a brief exchange of ideas for individual work, such as brainstorming initial ideas for individual work, provides the competitive student with personally rewarding group experiences before introducing activities which require working toward a group product and a group grade.

- Discussing the purposes for using small group learning may help students understand the benefits to their individual learning. Benefits might include: the importance of learning co-operative skills for life at home, at work, and in the community; and how the opportunity to discuss ideas with classmates contributes to individual learning. It may be helpful to reassure the student that group activity will not eliminate opportunity to work individually.

In rare situations, a student may experience great discomfort in working with others. This discomfort is often expressed in ways which disrupt learning for the individual and for the group. In these cases teachers can be most immediately supportive by providing the student with individual work. However, it is important to continue to provide the student with opportunities to participate in group work. Often teachers plan extra peer support, structure participation more closely, remove some of the academic pressure, assist the student in making a unique contribution, and provide a location for group work where the student feels most secure, for example, by holding group meetings around the student's desk.

It is important for teachers to provide the class with reasons why participation in group work is beneficial. People learn more effectively in co-operative groups because they articulate what they know and how they know. It is by talking through ideas that people think through ideas and reach deeper levels of understanding. Further, heterogeneity in groups provides a diversity of viewpoints and insights which contributes to the learning of everyone. The synergy that occurs in well-functioning groups builds understanding which very few people could achieve individually.

One Teacher's Experience

The following illustration shows how observation and supportive intervention can help students work together more effectively. The teacher of a general-level business studies course was working with his class on the topic of nonverbal communication and its effects in the workplace.

The teacher asked students to work in pairs to read and discuss a textbook article on nonverbal communication entitled "Soften is Password to Better Social Contact." Pairs then created a chart listing nonverbal messages that invite communication and nonverbal messages that discourage communication. Next, the teacher asked each pair to combine with another pair to discuss their charts. Using the ideas from their charts, the groups of four were to work together to design a poster featuring the nonverbals signals represented in the acronym SOFTEN.

One of the groups of four had a very difficult time working together. As the teacher moved about the class he observed physical evidence of the trouble. Group members were leaning out and away from each other; chairs were pulled back; individual members were re-reading the article or looking at the charts; there was little talking; arms were crossed and heads were down. Moving closer, the teacher heard the students worrying together about not being artistic and about not being able to design an attractive poster. The teacher wondered how he could help without intervening directly. He wanted the group to have an opportunity to solve its own problem.

Suddenly the teacher called out the words, "FREEZE! PLEASE DON'T ANYONE MOVE!" Surprised, students stayed perfectly still while the teacher asked them to examine the physical appearance of their group, to identify the nonverbal messages withing the group setting, and to compare those messages with how the work was going. In the following discussion the class was able to make two quick lists on the blackboard, a list of the nonverbal messages that may invite productive group work and a list of the nonverbal messages that may inhibit productive group work.

Then all the groups returned to their task. The teacher watched inconspicuously as the students in the group that was having trouble talked about their physical arrangement and decided to make changes. The group members pulled their chairs closer together, lifted their heads and leaned slightly forward. After a short discussion members decided on a simple design. They would place the letters of the word SOFTEN across the poster sheet and draw simple additions to the letters to represent the ideas from the article. The S became a smile; the O turned into a large eye with beguiling eyelashes; the F turned into a hand touching someone's shoulder; the E leaned forward with open arms, and the N looked as if it were moving up and down to represent a head nodding. Each group member helped to decorate the letters.

The teacher waited until the poster was nearly finished to join the group and asked students what they had learned about nonverbal communication from their experience of working together. The comment of one student said it all: "We had trouble getting anywhere until we actually put our heads together."

In the above case the teacher observed globally to get a sense of how the groups were working. Reflecting on the problem the one group was having, he devised a supportive intervention that furthered the academic learning while it assisted the group to solve its problem. Moreover, the intervention did not draw the attention of the rest of the class to the group or appear to judge the group unfavourably. Instead, it provided an opportunity for the group to attend to its own situation in a constructive manner. The teacher followed up the first intervention with further unobtrusive observation and then intervened a second time to help the group summarize what members had learned through the experience.

Summary

In this chapter we have examined two key elements of the teacher's role — observation and supportive intervention. Co-operative small group learning frees the teacher to fulfill these elements to a greater degree than traditional large group and individualized instructional methods. Observation provides a basis for understanding student needs and for planning supportive intervention.

Observation Form

Record examples of what group members do and say.

Group:_____ Date: _____

Names	Encouraging	Checking for Understanding	Sharing Ideas and Information

Observation Form

Place check marks in the appropriate boxes as you watch and listen. You might also want to record a few examples of what group members do or say.

	Asking Questions	Seeking Information and Opinions	Responding to Ideas	Acknowledging Contributions
Group 1				
Group 2				
Group 3				
Group 4				
Group 5				

Date _____

Observation Form

Record examples of students use of the co-operative skill: SHARING
INFORMATION AND IDEAS.

Sharing Information and Ideas	
Sounds Like	*Examples*
Looks Like	

7 Evaluating Group Work

Successful co-operative learning activities are dependent upon an interplay of these five principles.

1. Students work in positive interdependence.

2. Students work in small heterogeneous groups.

3. Students are accountable both as individuals and as a group.

4. Students learn through ample opportunity for purposeful talk.

5. Students learn and practise co-operative skills as they study and explore the subject matter together.

These principles are introduced in Chapter One and included as part of discussion in Chapter Two. Chapters Three and Four demonstrate how the principles work in practical application. Chapters Five and Six provide information on the teaching of co-operative skills. Chapter Seven describes evaluation methods.

Co-operative learning helps reduce math anxiety. I used to use group work a little and only for shorter tasks. Now I am using group work for more difficult and larger tasks that students were reluctant to attempt on their own. The students felt more comfortable in a small group and felt they got more help. I could point out the similarities and differences in the strategies used by different groups.

Secondary Teacher of Mathematics

Co-operative learning allows individuals to ferret out the particular skills of group members. My students learn how to use one another as resources and they do not depend on me as much.

Elementary Teacher

It's exciting when you see the students go further with ideas than you expect and see them apply skills they learned before.

Teacher of Adult Education

Evaluating Group Work

When co-operative group learning approaches are unfamiliar, teachers may feel unsure initially about how to evaluate. Often evaluation methods the teacher is already using can be adapted to this situation. As teachers find co-operative learning activities and evaluation methods that work for them, evaluation will become more comfortable.

Teachers employ evaluation methods suited to the co-operative learning activities they use. The amount of depth and time involved in evaluation should be proportionate to the intensity and duration of the co-operative learning activity. Teacher comments and student reflection at the end of a group activity is appropriate evaluation when the co-operative activity is brief. When groups work together for longer periods, such as in Extended Jigsaw or Group Investigation, evaluation should be an ongoing component of the learning process and should include evaluation of both learning processes and outcomes.

Research evidence supports the importance of rewarding both the individual contributions and the group product to assure participation by all students. Meaningful rewards include encouragement and praise as well as grades. With experience, the co-operative learning process itself becomes intrinsically rewarding. Students derive satisfaction from the assistance and support they get from their group members. The feelings of belonging and of being needed help group members to feel accountable to themselves and to their group.

As with all methodologies, evaluation practices need to be modified by the teacher to suit particular students and subject areas. It may be reassuring to keep in mind that the principles which guide good evaluation in individual or whole class learning can also help the teacher evaluate in the small group setting.

This chapter provides information regarding formative and summative evaluation of co-operative small group work. Four brief examples and two case studies of evaluation at the end of the chapter illustrate how teachers use the information to make evaluation integral to the learning experience. The chapter begins with an overview chart of themes in evaluation followed by questions which teachers frequently ask about evaluating group work.

Themes in Evaluating
Co-operative Small Group Work

WHY

- To identify students' initial interests and ideas about the topic
- To help students set daily goals

- To identify learning progress
- To identify where the teacher's help is needed
- To determine which parts of the learning activity are working well and which parts need modification

- To help students to reflect on their interests and learning outcomes
- To identify future learning objectives

WHAT

- Practising curriculum skills
- Applying concepts to solve new problems
- Organizational and thinking skills
- Co-operative interaction skills

**Evaluation
in
Co-operative
Learning**

BY WHOM

- The teacher
- The group
- The individual students

WHEN

- During the learning process

- At the end of a learning activity or unit of study

HOW

- Group progress reports and work plans
- Anecdotal descriptions of learning
- Quizzes and worksheets
- Observation of groups at work
- Group interaction checklists and reports
- Group discussions
- Projects, presentations
- Tests

Questions Teachers Ask

1. What is a good way to introduce evaluation when co-operative learning is new for students?

A way to ease into evaluation as students are learning to work in groups is to start by evaluating individual learning. Teachers can begin with informal co-operative learning activities such as those suggested in Chapter Two of this handbook. These brief co-operative activities directly assist individual learning. They provide opportunities for students to develop co-operative skills before being given the responsibility of creating a group product. Students will develop positive attitudes about group work if they first experience how group work enhances individual progress.

The learning which takes place during these informal opportunities can be evaluated through individual assignments such as reports, diagrams, models or quizzes.

Sample Informal Pair Activity to Enhance Individual Learning

- Before you start this assignment individually, discuss the questions with your partner to help each other understand what is being asked in each question.

Sample Question for Discussion to Understand Benefits of Co-operation

- Look over your assignment. Can you find one question which you were better able to answer as a result of discussing the questions with your partner?

---

2. How do teachers start to involve students in planning and carrying out evaluation of group work?

Students' understanding of the criteria for productive learning is a first step in becoming involved in evaluation. The teacher can model good evaluation practice by providing a list of learning criteria as part of the introduction to a group activity. Additionally, the teacher can engage the students in whole class or small group discussion of how the criteria can serve as a guide throughout the learning process. Gradually the teacher can involve the students in selecting the criteria and planning how to use them as a guide.

Criteria may be stated in checklist or flow chart form. For example, a checklist could describe the components or characteristics of a group product or the subskills involved in learning a skill. A flow chart may describe stages in the process of planning, designing, and carrying out the group task. Writing space is usually provided on the checklist or flow chart for anecdotal response.

Sample Criteria Checklist Developed by the Teacher and Students for Summative Peer and Teacher Evaluation

Criteria for Effective Group Presentation to Review Concepts in Trigonometry

	Not at all				Thoroughly
The group:					
• appeared prepared and organized.	—	—	—	—	—
• was knowledgeable about their section.	—	—	—	—	—
• worked together as a group.	—	—	—	—	—
• encouraged active participation from the class.	—	—	—	—	—
• demonstrated patience and helpfulness.	—	—	—	—	—
• used a variety of teaching techniques.	—	—	—	—	—

One part of the presentation which was particularly helpful (and why):

One suggestion for improvement:

---

3. How do teachers introduce students to self-evaluation?

Once students understand the criteria for evaluation they can begin to apply them in self-evaluation. Group self-evaluation is a helpful way for students to begin self-evaluation. In the process of discussing and writing about their learning as a group, students develop skill in identifying what they have learned, and in describing how the learning came about.

Sample Questions for Group Self-evaluation

- What did your group learn about helping group work go smoothly?
- Describe an idea or point of view you learned from another group which helped to clarify your group's conclusions.
- Describe the problem-solving steps your group used to improve the quality of your report.

Students can start individual self-evaluation by reflecting on their contribution and personal learning during the brief informal co-operative activities mentioned in Chapter Two. The focus for reflection on group interaction might include skills such as helping, explaining, demonstrating, listening, discussing, and sharing. The focus for reflection on academic learning might include skills such as giving reasons for ideas, explaining clearly, thinking visually, and reporting concisely.

Sample Questions for Individual Self-evaluation

- Describe something you helped your partner to learn.
- Describe one skill you learned from your experience of peer tutoring and how you learned the skill.
- Describe one idea you learned from viewing and asking questions about your partner's project.

Self-evaluation in the form of anecdotal comments is more informative than assigning grades. Descriptive comments allow students to make purposeful connections between their actions and how well they met the criteria established for successful learning.

Because of the personal nature of self-evaluation, students should be informed beforehand if they are to discuss their self-evaluations with the group or if they are to hand them in to the teacher.

4. When and how should students start evaluating each other?

Students need a good deal of experience developing and applying criteria to evaluate their individual learning and the work of their own group before they start to evaluate their peers. Through practice in self-evaluation, students will develop competence and understanding of the learning skills which are being evaluated and they will learn to express constructive comments. When students have competence with these skills, peer evaluation may be introduced.

Questions to elicit positive comments on others' work is a constructive way to introduce peer evaluation. By offering constructive comments students provide information which will assist their peers in future learning. The questions should be related to the criteria for evaluation developed at the beginning of the co-operative learning activity.

Sample Questions for Anecdotal Peer Evaluation

- Describe ways in which the group captured your interest.
- What did you learn from hearing how the other group developed its plans?
- Comment on helpful ways in which this group organized their information.

5. How do I teach students to evaluate themselves and their peers fairly and realistically?

Discussing learning objectives and criteria for evaluation before students begin a learning task and periodically during extended tasks helps students to be realistic and precise in their self- and peer evaluation.

The use of checklists throughout a co-operative learning activity provides guidelines for progress. Completed checklists assist groups in modifying and extending their plans.

Sample Group Self-evaluation

	A little				A great deal
• We checked with peers to be sure that they understood the work.	—	—	—	—	—
• We practised our ability to work with others by listening and contributing ideas to the group.	—	—	—	—	—
• We demonstrated patience when explaining concepts to the group.	—	—	—	—	—
• We worked to create a clear presentation.	—	—	—	—	—
• We were responsible in sharing the work to be done.	—	—	—	—	—

• What do you feel your group was particularly effective in doing?

• What would you like your group to be more effective in doing in the future?

Teachers can meet with groups to discuss the checklists and anecdotal evaluation. Teachers can encourage students to use the information from completed checklists to make plans for further learning. If the teacher uses the same evaluation criteria that students use, the teacher's evaluation helps students learn to evaluate constructively and honestly.

6. When should teachers start giving grades for group work?

It is appropriate for the teacher to begin giving grades for group work when students can apply co-operative skills effectively to complete a piece of work in groups. If group grades are given before students understand the purposes and benefits of co-operative group learning, group interaction may deteriorate as the group members struggle with the co-operative effort required to create a group product.

As well as giving grades for the completion of a group task, the teacher can assign grades for the completion of self- and peer anecdotal or checklist evaluations. If the students are experienced with peer evaluation the teacher can grade the peer evaluations to provide feedback to the evaluators on the helpfulness of their response.

Students need a great deal of experience with anecdotal self- and peer evaluation before they will be able to assign meaningful grades to themselves or one another. Many teachers wait until students reach senior levels of secondary education before introducing students to grading the work of self and peers.

7. When should students be given a group grade and when should individual grades be given?

If group work is to result in a group product, it is important to give one grade to the group for its collaborative work. Evaluation of the group as one unit will reinforce students' awareness that they are collectively responsible for their work and interaction.

If group work is to result in an individual product, for example, when individuals write a test or an essay, it is important to grade individually.

If students are to make distinct individual contributions to a group product, for example, when individuals write separate sections of a group report, a combination of both individual and group evaluation should be used. If there are difficulties with all group members taking responsibility for the work, the teacher may wish to structure assignments which explicitly require individual contributions to a group product.

Individual grades may also be a combination of a group grade for the group product and an individual grade for performance on a test or assignment that measures individual learning. Individual and group grades can be combined in proportions previously discussed by the teacher and students. Research suggests that motivation is increased by grading both the group product and individual contributions.

It is important that the teacher and students discuss beforehand the way in which grades will be allocated.

Sample Mid-Term Evaluation in Visual Arts Course

1. Each student will submit his/her individual journal describing personal learning experiences related to the course. (30%)

2. Each student will submit his/her portfolio of individual studio work. (40%)

3. Each student will submit a record of his/her individual tasks and responsibilities in the two group projects completed to date. (30%)

8. What proportion of evaluation should be based on the learning process and what proportion on the final product?

When deciding whether to emphasize evaluation of the process or the product, teachers consider the purposes of the evaluation. What do the teacher and students want to know about the learning that is taking place? For example, if the group task requires learning new curriculum skills, the teacher and students will want to monitor the development of skills throughout the learning process. Therefore the teacher will emphasize ongoing evaluation of the learning process. Once students have developed skills the teacher may assign a group task so that students can apply their skills to create a product. At this time the teacher may emphasize evaluation of the products of the co-operative group learning activity.

Evaluation describes student learning related to learning objectives. For example, if students are learning how to make point-form notes as part of a research study, the teacher may decide to emphasize the evaluation of the point-form notes at various points during the study and give lesser emphasis to a final product. One reason the teacher places greater emphasis on the skill of making point-form notes is because this learning objective is the initial priority.

Emphasis on process or product in evaluation is also determined by length of the group task. When group work extends over time, evaluation of the learning process is important in order to monitor the development of student learning. The ongoing evaluation supports student learning and helps contribute to the quality of the group product.

9. To what extent should group work be reflected in final term grades?

If the teacher uses group work primarily for the purpose of peer sharing and assistance with individual work, grades will be based primarily on individual work. Evaluation of the group work will be anecdotal and informal.

If group work involves students working together to create group products which are graded, then these grades will contribute to individual students' final grade. The amount of the term work done in small groups will influence the weighting in the final grade. Teachers who use group work regularly do so about 25-30% of the time.

10. What combination of weighting should the teacher and student evaluations carry in assigning grades?

When group work and involvement in evaluation are fairly new to students, the teacher will give more weight to his/her own evaluation. The teacher's evaluation will serve as a model and guide for student evaluation. Once students become skilled in group learning and are experienced with conducting evaluation, teachers may move toward averaging student and teacher evaluation.

Sample Evaluation Weighting

The anecdotal group self-evaluation will be graded on how well the comments address the criteria listed and how helpful the comments are in reflecting the group's efforts and in setting future learning goals.

Anecdotal Group Self-evaluation	40%
Teacher Grade (with anecdotal comments)	60%

11. How do I evaluate the group and individuals when a student is absent or not participating?

To avoid the difficulty of evaluating group work when students are absent, many teachers plan group activities to occur within one class period. To build positive attitudes towards participation, teachers begin with brief co-operative learning activities in which students help and share ideas for their individual work. Many teachers use brief activities early in the year to give students opportunity to experience the personal benefits of working co-operatively. Gradually teachers incorporate longer and more complex tasks which can still occur within one class meeting time and can contribute to individual products.

Throughout these beginning activities, ongoing self- and group anecdotal evaluation helps teachers to spot nonparticipation difficulties early enough to encourage participation. Many teachers report that students who are typically reluctant become productively engaged in co-operative small group work because of very active involvement and peer support which co-operative learning encourages.

Research indicates that as students become comfortable working productively in groups, attendance gradually improves and teachers are able to plan more extensive co-operative group tasks which span more than one class period.

12. What are ways other than grades for evaluating group work?

While grades may indicate the level of academic performance, they do not provide information for understanding the development and dimensions of student learning that are important for students, teachers, and parents. Descriptive anecdotal feedback, group discussion, checklists, and journal writing are evaluation activities which provide a rich source of information about the learning that is taking place. These evaluation activities also provide information to help set directions for future learning.

Formative and Summative Evaluation

There are many purposes for evaluation. Evaluation is a means of assessing the progress of student learning and of identifying areas for further learning and teaching. Evaluation can be an avenue for communication between teacher and students. It can be an avenue for recognizing achievements, for offering encouragement, and for developing understanding of how learning processes affect learning outcomes.

While it is important to encourage students to strive for accomplishment which may be reflected in marks or grades, it is also important to encourage students' enthusiasm for further learning and understanding of how future learning tasks might be approached.

There are two kinds of evaluation. Summative evaluation assesses learning outcomes at the end of a unit of study. Teachers are accustomed to thinking of summative evaluation as assessing students' grasp of academic knowledge. Other learning outcomes should also be evaluated in co-operative small group learning. These include:

- development of organizational and thinking skills;
- development of co-operative skills;
- development of positive attitudes about oneself, peers, and about learning.

Formative evaluation is ongoing and may be used to diagnose difficulties and needs. It assesses the learning process throughout a unit of study. Co-operative small group learning emphasizes formative evaluation. Formative evaluation can help the teacher and students:

- develop deeper understandings of students' current skills, attitudes, and behaviour;
- modify or set new teaching or learning objectives;
- adapt the pace or form of learning activities.

The Process of Evaluation

The following chart depicts the process of evaluation in co-operative small group learning. Decisions about evaluation are made on the basis of learning objectives. Both formative and summative evaluation of academic learning and group interaction are involved. Formative evaluation may lead to new or revised learning objectives during a unit of study. Summative evaluation may identify future learning objectives. Students and teacher participate in all aspects of the evaluation process. Thus evaluation is collaborative and cyclical.

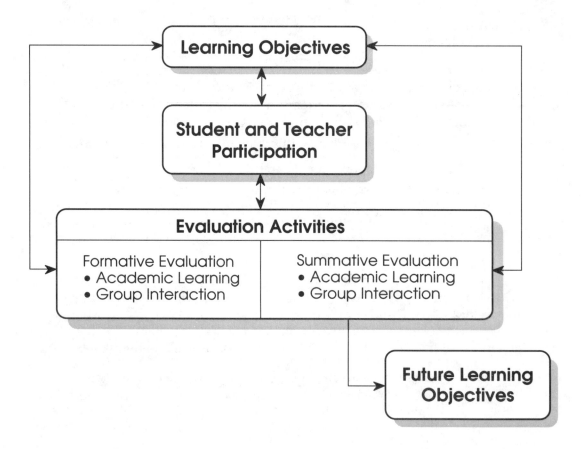

The remainder of this chapter explores the process of evaluation illustrated above. The next two sections examine ways of relating evaluation to learning objectives, and involving students in planning and carrying out evaluation. Suggestions for formative and summative evaluation activities follow. The four brief examples and the two case studies at the end of the chapter illustrate ways teachers can integrate all aspects of the evaluation process.

Relating Evaluation To Learning Objectives

Learning objectives state the learning outcomes expected of students. Decisions about what is to be evaluated and how it is to be evaluated are determined by learning objectives. They help the teacher to select evaluation activities that enable students to demonstrate the skills they have been learning. For example, if a learning objective in mathematics is to develop problem-solving skills, the teacher designs evaluation activities that encourage students to use and describe their problem-solving strategies. Problem solving will be given priority in evaluation over other skills which may be important at other times.

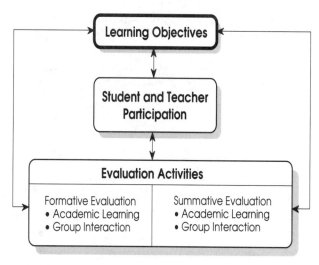

Similarly, if a learning objective is to practise open-ended, exploratory discussion, the teacher might assign an essay in which students explore and interpret a theme. Evaluating students' performance on this task encourages students to demonstrate the thinking skills developed during exploratory discussion, while a test that assesses the recall of facts would not.

When planning a unit of study which employs co-operative small groups, it is important to identify both academic and group interaction learning objectives. Good group interaction skills enable effective academic learning to occur among group members. For example, the skill of disagreeing in a pleasant way helps to invite risk-taking in discussion and fosters the development of critical thinking skills.

Making students aware of the learning objectives and how learning will be evaluated helps students to understand the purpose of learning activities and their desired outcomes. When several students work together in a small group activity, it is particularly important that all group members share an understanding of their learning objective.

Many learning activities involve several skills. If teachers find that students need to develop specific skills in order to accomplish the objective, then the specific skill also becomes a learning objective to be evaluated. For example, the objective may be to write an essay to develop a point of view with sequentially presented arguments and examples. In order for students to achieve this learning objective, the teacher may find it necessary initially to work on the specific skills of making point-form notes and an outline. The teacher will evaluate these skills as well as the finished essay.

The following examples illustrate possible learning objectives and sample co-operative learning activities for learning and evaluating the skills described in the objectives. Several objectives are given for each co-operative activity. The teacher may choose a particular objective to emphasize in evaluation. For example, if co-operative learning is new to students, the teacher may want to emphasize a co-operative skill in evaluation. If students have previously developed co-operative skills, the teacher may want to emphasize an academic skill in evaluation.

Criteria for evaluating students' accomplishment of a learning objective and sample methods for carrying out evaluation are provided later in the chapter.

Level: Primary
Subject: Science
Topic: Characteristics of Birds

Learning Objectives

- To practise sharing materials, contributing and listening to others' ideas.

- To learn to identify and classify characteristics of birds.

- To practise posing questions.

Co-operative Learning Activity

As part of a unit on birds, pairs cut out pictures of birds and group the pictures according to characteristics. For example, the students might classify the birds by size, shape, or characteristics of the beaks, feet, or wings. The pairs write questions about one of their groups of birds which they would like to explore as part of the unit of study.

Level: Junior
Subject: Social Studies
Topic: Famous People in History

Learning Objectives

- To develop student awareness that working co-operatively can assist individual learning.

- To identify main ideas from reading.

- To practise making point-form notes.

- To learn about the life and historical significance of a famous person.

Co-operative Learning Activity

All students individually read a short article on the same famous historical figure, for example, Alexander Bell, Amelia Erhart, Martin Luther King Jr., and Chief Dan George. Students note key points in what is read, such as: why the person is famous, educational background, and people who influenced the person. Pairs share their individual notes and expand or condense them with the help of the partner.

Level: Junior
Subject: Science
Topic: Learning About the Human Body

Learning Objectives

- To be able to describe functions of parts of the body.

- To develop the co-operative skills of helping and listening to others.

- To understand how parts of the body work as a team to keep the body healthy.

Co-operative Learning Activity

Using Jigsaw, each member in the home groups of four selects a different part of the body to study, for example, the heart, stomach, kidney or lung. In exploration groups of two, partners learn about the size, general structure, and function of the body part they are studying. In home groups, each member teaches what he/she has learned. The whole class and the teacher discuss how the functions of the parts of the body are interrelated.

Level: Junior/Intermediate
Subject: Language Skills
Topic: Getting to Know Classmates/Interviewing

Learning Ojectives

- To help students get to know classmates at the beginning of the year.

- To develop the interviewing skills of asking questions, listening, and recording information.

- To practise oral communication skills.

Co-operative Learning Activity

To prepare for interviewing, the teacher and whole class brainstorm a list of possible interview topics, for example, special interests, favourite books, the funniest thing that you ever experienced, and personal heroes and heroines. The teacher models the interviewing skills of asking questions, listening, and recording information.

The students interview each other in pairs. Pairs combine and each member gives a description of the student he/she interviewed. In discussion, the group identifies interests and experiences members have in common and an interest of each person the group would like to know more about.

Level: Junior/Intermediate
Subject: Geography
Topic: Map Skills

Learning Objectives

- To practise applying map symbols and location skills.

- To develop the thinking skill of making inferences.

- To practise narrative writing skills.

- To learn the co-operative skills of assigning individual responsibilities and synthesizing ideas in one written product.

Co-operative Learning Activity

In groups of four, the students have previously practised map reading using maps of countries being studied in the course. In the first phase of the present task, each group is asked to make a map of an imaginary continent and to include the map symbols previously learned.

In the second phase, the groups are to write an account of life on the imaginary continent based on the geography depicted in the map. Each group member selects a subtopic to prepare, for example, climate, industry, foods eaten, types of living dwellings, and popular forms of recreation. The group then synthesizes the subsections into one report for display in the classroom.

Level: Primary to Adult
Subject: English as a Second Language
Topic: Celebrations

Learning Objectives

- To provide opportunity for students to get to know each other.

- To practise oral communication skills in English.

- To identify and appreciate similarities and differences in family and cultural traditions.

Co-operative Learning Activity

The class brainstorms characteristics of celebrations, for example, the purpose of the celebration, people who participate, when the event takes place, food and decorations prepared. In pairs, each student interviews the other about a family celebration. Pairs combine to share their information and identify similarities and differences in their celebrations. A representative from each group reports the similarities and differences to the whole class. The combined class list forms the basis for a class discussion of the importance of cultural and family celebrations.

Level: Senior
Subject: Visual Arts
Topic: Movements in Painting

Learning Objectives

- To recall and apply knowledge of movements in painting through discussion with classmates.

- To analyze reproductions of paintings and to make inferences about stylistic characteristics.

- To practise the previously learned co-operative skills of sharing ideas, encouraging others, and making decisions based on the views of all.

Co-operative Learning Activity

In previously formed base groups of four, students review their knowledge of movements in painting, for example, realism and expressionism. The groups are asked to apply their knowledge to analyze two reproductions of paintings which they have not seen before. They are asked to identify the movement represented and to give reasons for their decision.

Involving Students in Planning and Carrying Out Evaluation

Evaluation should be a collaborative process involving students and teacher. Co-operative small group learning provides greater opportunity to involve students in planning and carrying out evaluation than do traditional full class or individual instruction. Small groups provide natural forums for students to discuss concerns and questions about evaluation practices. As students grow to feel accountable to themselves, to the teacher, and to their peers, they see evaluation as part of their learning process.

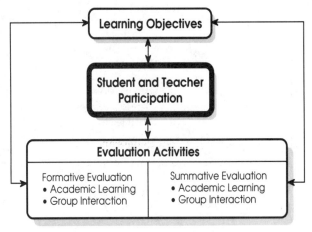

Involving Students in Planning Evaluation

At the beginning of a unit of study, the teacher involves students in planning by discussing the learning objectives with them. Class discussion of learning goals helps students to develop a purpose for working together. When groups of students understand the learning objectives, they are better able to work together to achieve them.

Often, students are not accustomed to thinking about learning objectives. Thinking about a learning objective includes identifying criteria that will indicate success in meeting the objective. The teacher gradually involves students in planning some of the criteria on which learning will be evaluated. For example, teacher and students together may develop a checklist of criteria which describes the components or characteristics of a successful final product. The checklist may describe components or steps in a process, for example, a list of skills for working effectively in an instrumental ensemble.

Sample Checklist of Skills for
Working Effectively in an Ensemble

Working together in an ensemble requires the co-operation and responsible effort of every section member. This checklist contains criteria which we have developed together. Sectional groups will meet twice monthly to complete the checklist below.

Never   *Always*

Preparing
Are we following the guidelines for independent practice?

Are we arriving on time?

Are we bringing our folders and pencils?

Are we opening our cases on the floor at the back of the room?

Are we putting our instruments together quietly and carefully?

Are we taking our places quickly to be ready for the first cue?

Playing
Are we assuming correct posture?

Are we following the conductor with complete attention?

Are we listening actively to our own playing and that of other sections?

Are we waiting patiently while others play?

Are we encouraging others within our section?

Closing
Are we noting trouble spots for independent practice?

Are we putting our instruments away carefully and quietly?

Are we checking to see if our help is needed to take down the chairs and stands?

Are we signing the *Take out sheets* before leaving?

Are we leaving the classroom in an orderly and responsible fashion?

Our Goal for Improvement:

_____

_____

_____

Date: _____ **Signatures:** _____

The teacher can involve students in discussion about evaluation plans. Students can assist the teacher to make some of the decisions. The class can talk about questions such as the following.

- Who will evaluate?
- What kinds of learning activities will be evaluated?
- How will the evaluation be conducted? How will grades be determined from the evaluation?
- When will evaluation take place?

By assisting the teacher in making the "who," "what," "how," and "when" kinds of decisions about evaluation, students develop responsibility for their own learning and for the learning of others. Class discussion of evaluation methods informs the teacher of learning outcomes which students see as important. It is valuable to include in evaluation those learning outcomes which were not anticipated at the outset of a unit of study.

Involving Students in Carrying Out Evaluation

The teacher also involves students in carrying out evaluation. While students are learning how to participate in evaluation, it is not advisable to ask them to assign marks to their own work or to the work of peers. Even in advanced grades, unless students have significant experience in peer and self-evaluation it is unrealistic to expect them to assign marks or have marks assigned to them by other students.

A useful way to begin to involve students in carrying out evaluation is through anecdotal group self-evaluation. Group self-evaluation may be easier for students than beginning with individual self-evaluation or peer evaluation. Groups can make comments on their own progress, for example, on tasks they completed, skills they learned, understandings they developed and skills they would like to improve. The discussion that occurs as group members work together to write anecdotal comments helps students to develop the skill of reflecting on experience. Following are sample evaluation questions to encourage group reflection.

Sample questions for group self-evaluation

- Describe something that people in your group learned which you could not have learned working alone.
- Design one question for the test which you think will encourage other groups to consider important ideas on the topic your group presented.
- What did you learn from describing your group's work to the other group?
- Describe the problem-solving steps your group used to improve the school dance (or study skills, getting along in the playground, and so on).

Once students become familiar with group self-evaluation, groups can be encouraged to offer constructive anecdotal comments on the work of other groups. The form that follows is one way teachers can involve groups in this activity.

Sample Evaluation of Another Group's Presentation

- How did the group capture your interest in the topic?

- Describe three things you learned about the topic from the presentation.

- Describe one thing about the presentation that you thought was creative or imaginative.

- Make one suggestion which you think would strengthen the effectiveness of the presentation.

- Was there anything about the presentation which makes you interested in learning more about the topic? If so, please indicate what it was.

Names _____

Anecdotal peer evaluation becomes meaningful to students when learning in co-operative groups. Because small group work provides opportunity to observe and discuss learning strategies with peers, students learn effective strategies from each other. Because of the intimate nature of small groups, students develop understanding of the successes and struggles of their peers. As stereotypes dissolve in the process of working closely together, peer evaluation tends to be sensitive and constructive.

Formative Evaluation

Evaluating Academic Learning

Formative evaluation occurs throughout a learning activity and informs the teacher of the groups' progress. Formative evaluation also helps groups to identify their accomplishments and tasks or skills which will improve their work. Sample activities for formative evaluation of academic learning are provided in the chart on the next page.

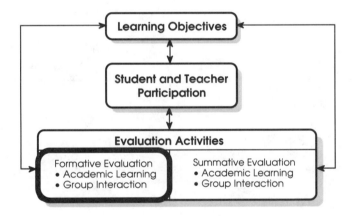

Sample Activities for Formative Evaluation of Academic Learning

- Checklists of tasks completed, tasks to do

- Early drafts of writing; early drafts with group's suggestions for reshaping or editing

- Inventories of materials needed

- Lists of initial ideas generated from brainstorming

- Outlines

- Progress reports

- Quizzes

- Response journals

- Self and group anecdotal reports of concepts understood, procedures mastered, procedures for which the group needs assistance

- Worksheets

- Discussions

- Evaluation of effort as well as accomplishment

- Learning logs

- Observation of rehearsals

- Point form notes

- Plans, flowcharts

- Sketches for artwork or constructions

- Teacher or peer conferences with the group to assess progress and to set future goals

- Work habit profiles

Following are four kinds of formative evaluation activities which can be used to assess academic learning.

Action Plans and Progress Reports

Action plans and progress reports focus on the work students are doing. They help teacher and students to set goals and time lines, and to assess progress. Action plans and progress reports encourage the development of planning and decision-making skills and the co-ordination of all group members' efforts. They inform the teacher of where assistance may be needed.

The following kinds of action plans and progress reports can be handed in by groups and evaluated by the teacher on specified target dates:

- overall plans for the work;
- outlines of final reports;
- rough drafts of final reports;
- lists of tasks for which individual group members are responsible;
- checklists of the steps to be completed during the group work.

Sample Progress Report

- Work our group has completed

_____

_____

_____

- Work our group has yet to do

_____

_____

_____

- Individual members' responsibilities

_____

_____

_____

- A task with which our group could use help

_____

_____

_____

Quizzes and Worksheets

Quizzes and worksheets provide opportunity to practise skills and learn facts. Knowing in advance when a quiz will occur provides a goal for groups to work towards. The completed quiz or worksheet provides feedback on the progress of learning. Students can participate in creating worksheet questions for their own group members or for other groups.

Co-operative quizzes and co-operative worksheets offer pairs or groups the opportunity to review curriculum concepts. Group members can take practice quizzes together and subsequently analyze where members need to concentrate attention for improvement.

Monitoring in Base Groups

Base groups, which are described in Chapter Three, can provide ongoing evaluation of skills, such as note-taking skills, study skills, homework skills, and writing skills. For example, the teacher and students may have developed a checklist of criteria for good homework practices. In their groups, students use the checklist to interview each other and make suggestions.

Through these kinds of monitoring activities, students become proficient in analyzing their strengths and weaknesses and in setting new learning goals. When a group shares the responsibility for each member's learning, students support and assist each other's efforts to improve.

Sample forms for formative evaluation are included in the two case studies at the end of the chapter. The following sample questions encourage students to reflect on their learning and on how to provide assistance to group members.

Sample Questions to Encourage Reflection

- Describe one part of your work that seems to require help from your group.
- Describe one strategy for doing homework (or, making a plan, revising an essay) that works for you and that might be helpful to others in your group.
- Describing one thing you learned about mixing colours (or, using a microscope) from teaching the skill to your group.
- Describe two things you learned about study skills (or, planning your project) from listening to the report of the steering committee.

Teacher Observation and Feedback

Teacher Observation and feedback also provide information on the progress of learning. Information on teacher observation is included in Chapter Six. Teacher observation is not only a means of assessing students' learning; observation also gives teachers confidence that their use of small group learning is effective. The following sample questions may guide teacher observation and group discussion.

A sample Teacher Observation Form is included in the History Case Study, p. 191.

Evaluating Group Interaction

In co-operative small group learning, group interaction should be evaluated on a frequent basis. Group self-evaluation helps students to assess their own progress in learning to work with others and develops awareness of co-operative skills that will help the group function more effectively. Academic learning improves as the quality of group interaction improves. Group self-evaluation should be in the form of constructive comments

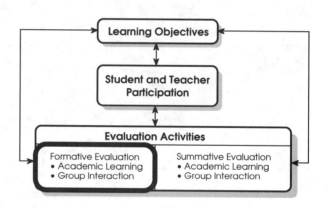

rather than in the form of marks. Marks do not provide information about how to improve. Asking groups to describe goals and behaviours which may improve their functioning helps students to think constructively about their group interaction.

The following examples describe four formative evaluation activities which can be used to assess group interaction.

Checklists and Questions

Checklists and questions help students to become aware of accomplishments and difficulties in working together. Sample checklists are provided in Chapter Five and in the History and Science case studies at the end of this chapter.

Teacher Observation and Review

Observing groups and reviewing their progress checklists help the teacher to see how group interaction is affecting the academic work. Based on this information, the teacher can ask questions which help groups to improve their effectiveness. For example, saying, "It sounds like a few people are doing most of the talking. Are you encouraging everyone to contribute ideas before you make decisions?" draws the group's attention to a strategy that could enhance group functioning.

Constructive comments from the teacher to individuals and to groups can have several positive effects. They convey the message that difficulties are understood. They suggest ways of coping with them. They foster students' motivation to learn from their difficulties. They serve as a model for students' interaction.

Discussion

Class or small group discussion helps teach students to assess group interaction.

Sample Topics for Group Discussion

- Organizing and using work time effectively
- Fulfilling individual work responsibilities
- Encouraging and helping group members
- Resolving conflicts among group members

Discussions may be brief or extended. Students in different groups may exchange successful strategies. During extended group activities regular opportunities for discussion are especially important. Discussion can also focus on understanding and solving a problem which a group cannot readily solve without assistance. When sensitive issues arise, the teacher will want to facilitate constructive discussion that leads to problem solving.

The Teacher's Role In Facilitating Constructive Discussions

- Act as facilitator rather than as problem solver.
- Intervene with an attitude of caring, gentleness, and patience.
- Encourage all group members to contribute to describing the problem.
- Reflect back concerns expressed by group members.
  "It sounds as if the group is concerned about..."
  "It sounds as if the group would like to be able to..."
- Encourage students to offer solutions. The teacher may also encourage suggestions from other groups which have experienced and found solutions to a similar problem.
- Encourage the group to try a solution which would satisfy all members.
- After the group has had opportunity to try a solution, enquire whether the group is satisfied.

Open-Ended Statements

Asking groups to complete open-ended statements such as: "Our suggestions for improvement are..." or "Group members helped in the planning stages by..." assists students to think about their group interaction skills. Completing open-ended statements encourages students to apply their thinking skills to solve group difficulties. Students can learn to describe why they think a success or problem occurred and can consider different points of view and solutions to difficulties. The following illustrates how one group completed an open ended statement.

At the beginning we couldn't get anywhere because we just kept talking about our own ideas and didn't listen to each other. After the class discussion about sharing leadership, we listened to each other more and were able to put different people's ideas together.

> ### Sample Open-Ended Statements
> ### When a Problem Occurs
>
> - *The problem is...*
> - *When this problem occurs, I/other group members feel...*
> - *A solution to this problem might be...*
> - *If we tried this solution, our group would be able to...*
> - *If we tried this solution, I/other group members would feel...*

Teachers should emphasize the importance of sensitivity to others' feelings when identifying and solving problems. Problem solving in groups does not involve blaming or judging others. The emphasis instead is on understanding one's own and others' feelings, and on what "we" can do to help our group function well.

Summative Evaluation

Evaluating Academic Learning

Summative evaluation occurs at the end of a learning activity or unit of study. Evaluation may be based on the development of academic skills which occurred during the learning activity or unit, as well as on a completed product or test to assess learning outcomes.

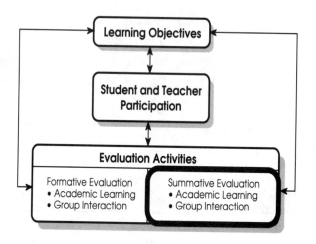

When planning summative evaluation, the teacher needs to decide when to evaluate individual work and when to evaluate group work. Both forms of evaluation are important. Research indicates that students are highly motivated to do their best work as individual learners and as team members when they know that both kinds of effort "count" toward their final mark on a unit of study.

The following is a summary of suggestions to help the teacher decide when to evaluate individual work and when to evaluate group work. These suggestions are also discussed on p. 143.

- If group work results in a group product, for example, a group presentation, it is important to give one grade to the group for its collaborative work.

- If group work results in individual products, for example, when individuals write a test or complete an assignment, it is important to grade individually.

- If students make distinct individual contributions to a group product, for example, when individuals write separate sections of a group report, a combination of both individual and group evaluation should be used.

- Individual grades may be a combination of a group grade for the group product and an individual grade for performance on a test or assignment at the end of the learning activity.

- It is important that the teacher and students discuss beforehand the way in which grades will be allocated.

Sample activities for evaluating academic learning outcomes are provided in the chart below.

Sample Activities for Summative Evaluation of Academic Learning

- Annotated scrapbooks

- Critiques

- Debates

- Drama, mime, and musical performances

- Flowcharts depicting processess in science, mathematics investigation

- Panel discussions

- Tests to assess factual recall, problem solving, interpreting events, describing a point of view

- Visual arts creations, murals, photo documents, dioramas, crafts

- Anthologies of the group's creative writings (poetry, stories, dialogues)

- Demonstrations

- Essays

- Multi-media presentations

- Oral reports

- Portfolios

- Written reports

An advantage of co-operative small group learning is that it provides greater opportunity for students to be involved in carrying out evaluation. Following are three suggestions for involving groups in summative evaluation of academic learning.

Groups Design Evaluation Tasks for Themselves

Groups can design evaluation tasks for themselves. For example, the teacher may design two open-ended questions for a test and ask each group to design a third question members would like to answer in order to demonstrate their learning. The experience of designing the question at the end of a unit of study encourages the group to review and reflect on what members have learned.

Groups Design Evaluation Tasks for Others

Groups can design evaluation tasks for other students. If each group has given a presentation on a different subtopic, each group can design an appropriate task to assess the learning of others regarding that subtopic. The responses of other students also help each group to assess the effectiveness of its presentation and its evaluation task.

Students Evaluate Their Own Learning

Students can be encouraged to describe their own learning through journal writing and in conferences with the teacher. Portfolios or learning contracts also provide a focus for student self-evaluation.

Self-evaluation is particularly valuable after group work which has involved analysis and interpretation of ideas. This kind of work stimulates students' thinking and may result in personal learning which is not evident in performance of tasks which the teacher assigns. Talking with peers to clarify what has been learned enables students to articulate their personal learning and to become aware of the processes by which they learn.

Sample Questions for Self-Evaluation

- Describe something you learned about (solving a mathematical problem/understanding a poem/writing an essay) from working with your group members.
- What conclusions did you reach about your topic as a result of your group discussions?
- How would you improve your next project report?

The following self-evaluation comments illustrate what three students learned during co-operative learning experiences.

I used to think that I could not relate to poetry because I thought the only one that could understand it was someone creative or imaginative. However, I learned that everyone can relate to poetry because as long as you are experiencing life, then you are experiencing poetry. I now look at poetry as being the natural way of recording important experiences or thoughts that occur during life.

I always thought poetry was boring. The discussions helped me to express my feelings. I learned to appreciate the poem and actually got a sense of what it was trying to say.

We learn more English by discussing the story in groups. Group work gave us the opportunity to speak out and get out of our shyness. We got to know each other and we combined our opinions in English. Sometimes it is hard to get our ideas out because of our level of English. In the small group we helped each other with English words and had a chance to hear different ideas about the ending of the story.

Evaluating Group Interaction

Summative evaluation of group interaction is a new experience for most teachers. This kind of evaluation helps the teacher to plan future group activities. It fosters students' understanding of their personal and social development, including their development of positive attitudes and co-operative skills. The teacher should involve students in the process of planning and carrying out the evaluation of group interaction outcomes.

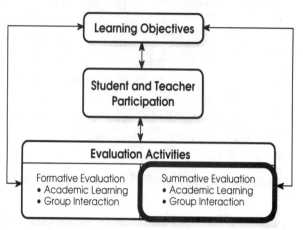

Following are three suggestions for summative evaluation of group interaction. More ideas are provided in Chapter Five and in the four examples and two case studies at the end of this chapter.

Groups Evaluate Their Effectiveness

The teacher can ask the group to evaluate its interaction skills. Students can individually assess the group interaction and then hold a group discussion to reach a collective assessment. Student analysis of group interaction offers the teacher insight into the growth which has taken place.

Teachers can encourage students to consider how their group interaction affected the academic work. The following types of questions encourage this kind of reflection.

Sample Questions to Assess Group Functioning

- What problems did your group have in working together?
- What solutions did your group suggest?
- How did the solution you chose make work easier?
- Would you use it again? Why?

Students Evaluate Their Own Group Interaction Skills

During group work, members become aware of their strengths and difficulties in working co-operatively. Sometimes members set personal goals for developing co-operative skills. Self-evaluation provides an opportunity for students to describe personal goals, levels of confidence, and their own understanding of how their co-operative skills affected group interaction.

Because of the personal nature of this kind of reflection, confidentiality is important. Students should know at the outset whether they will be expected to discuss this evaluation with their group or hand it in to the teacher.

Sample Questions for Self-Evaluation

- Did you learn anything about yourself while working in this group? If so, what did you learn?
- What were your strengths in working co-operatively in the group?
- What co-operative skills would you like to improve next time you work in a group?

The following illustrates what one student learned about herself during a co-operative learning experience.

> *By the end I learned I'm not too good at taking suggestions. Working in that group helped me overcome the need to take control.*

Teachers should read students' descriptions of their personal learning before the teacher conducts summative evaluation of group interaction. If teacher evaluation is conducted after students evaluate themselves, the teacher can provide feedback which responds to the issues which are important to the particular student or group.

The Teacher Provides Constructive Comments

The teacher can help students evaluate group interaction by reporting links between students' accounts of their group interaction and the quality of the completed group or individual work.

Written comments and questions that convey interest in students' successes and difficulties can make evaluation a form of personal communication and may encourage students to work on areas of difficulty in the future. The following comments illustrate one teacher's constructive approach to summative evaluation of group interaction.

Sample Comments from the Teacher

- *Alex, I was very pleased by the increase in your ease in a group. You came a long way on this one.*
- *Your group appeared well organized as you made your report. Each member had a role to play. The transitions between presentations were effective.*
- *Nora, earlier you sounded worried about doing an oral presentation with your group. The presentation went well. You sounded confident.*
- *Your group self-evaluation indicated that you experienced some confusion when it came time to put your written reports together. I think your suggestion for next time is right — more effective planning at the beginning would help.*

Constructive personal comments such as those above can have several positive effects. They convey the message that difficulties will be responded to with understanding and constructive suggestions. They foster students' motivation to learn from difficulties. They serve as a model for students' interaction with each other.

Four Examples of Evaluation

The four examples which follow demonstrate different methods for evaluating small group work. The examples illustrate how different evaluation activities may be appropriate for different learning objectives, student needs, and kinds of co-operative learning tasks. When co-operative learning is new to students, the group tasks are brief. Emphasis is placed on informal formative evaluation of the group learning process and on summative evaluation of individual learning.

When students are experienced with group learning, extended co-operative learning activities are introduced. In these activities, summative evaluation includes evaluation of group products as well as individual learning. When students have had prior experience with self-evaluation, they participate in designing evaluation tasks and peer evaluation is introduced.

Level: Primary
Subject: Language Study

Teacher's Purpose and the Co-operative Learning Activity
The teacher introduces small group learning during the daily story time while reading to the class. She pauses several times at eventful moments in the story and asks the students to turn to a classmate sitting next to them. Partners are asked to take two minutes to exchange ideas on what might happen next in the story, on what a character may be feeling, or a personal experience related to a story event. After each pause for sharing in pairs, the teacher asks four different students to share their ideas with the whole class.

Learning Objectives
1. To learn the co-operative skills of taking turns and listening.

2. To practise making predictions and relate story events to personal experience.

Formative Evaluation
1. While the pairs are sharing ideas, the teacher observes for signs of involvement, taking turns and listening, for example, one person talking at a time, seeing heads together, nodding, smiling. To encourage the students to become aware of their co-operative skills, the teacher briefly comments on examples of how she saw pairs listening and taking turns.

2. As the four students report their ideas to the whole class, the teacher encourages students to give reasons for their ideas. The teacher accepts all ideas, as the objective is to encourage the students' thinking rather than to predict the author's thinking.

Summative Evaluation
As the co-operative activity is brief and informal to introduce students to small group learning, there is no summative evaluation; however, the teacher could encourage the students to use ideas shared in individual drawing or writing activities about the story.

Level: Junior
Subject: Social Studies

The Teacher's Purpose and the Co-operative Learning Activity
The teacher assigns the following task to help students experience personal benefits from working co-operatively. In the following task students help each other with their individual work. All students individually read a short article on the same famous historical figure (for example, Alexander Graham Bell, Amelia Erhart, Martin Luther King Jr.) and note key points in what is read (for example, why the person is famous, talents, people who influenced the person). Pairs share their individual notes and expand or condense them with the help of the partner.

Learning Objectives
1. To develop awareness that working co-operatively can assist individual learning.
2. To identify main ideas from reading.
3. To develop the skill of making point form notes.
4. To learn about the life and historical significance of a famous person.

Formative Evaluation
Because the co-operative task is brief, evaluation is informal.

1. Before the pairs meet, the teacher and students identify criteria for helping others. The students suggest the following helping behaviours: taking turns, listening to others' ideas, and making constructive suggestions. These behaviours suggested by the students become the criteria for evaluating co-operative skills.
2. After pairs have shared and revised their notes, they discuss how well they took turns, listened, and offered constructive suggestions.
3. The students are asked to reflect individually on how working with a partner was helpful. Each student also completes the following sentence stem: "Something I learned from my partner about finding main ideas or making point form notes was . . ."
4. Students hand in their point-form notes to the teacher who responds with comments and suggestions. The notes handed in help the teacher to set the next learning objectives. The teacher decides that the class needs further assistance and practice in reading for main ideas and in making point-form notes.
5. When the students have developed the skills of reading for meaning and making point-form notes, the teacher will set a new learning objective: to apply these skills in making oral presentations. Each student will choose an historical figure to research and make a two-minute presentation to the class. In preparation for the presentation, the students will make point-form notes on what they want to say. They will review their notes and practise their oral presentation with their partner.

Summative Evaluation
Summative evaluation will be based on the work on the presentations.
1. Partners will discuss how their notes helped in preparing their presentations.
2. The teacher will provide supportive comments and suggestions on the presentations.

Level: Primary to Adult
Subject: English as a Second Language

The Teacher's Purpose and the Co-operative Learning Activity
The teacher uses the following one-week activity to help the students get to know each other and to develop their confidence about communicating in English. The teacher chooses the theme "Celebrating Special Days" so the students will have opportunity to share knowledge from their personal experience.

On the first day, the class brainstorms characteristics of celebrations, for example, the reason for the celebration, activities which occur, people who particpate, and food and decorations prepared. Each student develops questions to interview a classmate on an occasion that her/his family celebrates in spring. On the second day, pairs of students interview each other about a family or cultural celebration. On the third day, pairs combine to share their information and to identify the similarities and differences in the accounts. On the fourth day, a representative from each group reports the similarities and differences to the whole class. With the teacher's assistance, the class discusses the importance of family and cultural celebrations.

Learning Objectives
1. To provide opportunity for students to get to know classmates by sharing personal knowledge.
2. To practice oral communication skills in English.
3. To develop co-operative skills. The students identified the following skills as important for their interviewing and discussion activities: listening with interest, asking questions to understand what another is saying, and helping each other with English.
4. To appreciate similarities and differences among cultures and the importance of family and cultural traditions.

Formative Evaluation
1. After the interviews, partners exchange comments on how their partner's use of one of the co-operative skills put them at ease while being interviewed. The students are encouraged to use these skills again when the pairs combine to work as a group of four.
2. During the group work, the teacher moves about the room, watching and listening from a distance for the three co-operative skills. Because the primary learning objectives are for students to get to know each other and to practise speaking English in a small peer group, the teacher does not want to disrupt the spontaneity of peer interaction unless a group cannot continue without assistance.

Summative Evaluation

1. At the end of the week's activity, the groups of four use a three-point rating scale (seldom, some of the time, often) to evaluate their use of the three co-operative skills.
2. Individually, the students write comments on something interesting that they learned about their partner's celebration and a way their group of four helped someone with English.

The following evaluation activities could be used with secondary school classes.

3. The students receive a group mark out of five for the variety of ways in which they classified similarities and differences among their celebrations.
4. The students receive an individual mark out of five for the following homework assignment completed at the end of the week: each student writes a one-page description of the importance and symbolic meaning of family and cultural celebrations.

Level: Senior
Subject: Mathematics

Teacher's Purpose and the Co-operative Learning Activity
In a three-week unit on statistics, the teacher uses base groups on a daily basis to provide peer support for learning about statistics; to encourage a broader understanding of statistics as methods for explaining and predicting behaviour or events; and to foster awareness of the potential for error in the interpretation of statistics.

For ten minutes at the beginning of the period, group members share their completed homework. In their groups, students explain how they developed their solutions to statistics problems. They share effective strategies, for example, restating the problem in other ways, making an educated guess about expected outcomes, discovering new problem-solving strategies, visualizing problems and drawing graphs, tables and diagrams to depict information. This discussion of strategies is designed to develop students' awareness that a variety of skills can be employed in problem solving. The groups also discuss how the statistical concepts are applied in society.

Ten minutes before the end of the period, after whole class instruction, students return to their base groups to summarize the concepts taught.

Learning Objectives
1. To increase interest in learning about statistics and the role of statistics in society.
2. To develop students' awareness of their problem-solving skills and the ability to describe their problem-solving process (metacognition).
3. To practise the co-operative skills of contributing, checking for understanding, listening to understand others' ideas and demonstrating patience in helping others.

Formative Evaluation
1. The teacher observes groups at work for signs of increased interest, for example, staying on task, contribution of ideas from all members, fewer requests for assistance from the teacher.
2. Once during the unit, each group does a demonstration for the class. The group demonstrates the solution to one homework question, describes the strategies their group members used to find the solution and discusses an application of the statistic in society. The following peer evaluation is carried out to assist the presenting group in preparing for future demonstrations. Classmates respond to the following questions:
    (1) Comment on one aspect of the demonstration which helped you understand the problem and solution for example, stating the problem clearly, explaining the steps in the solution sequentially, using diagrams, and providing interesting examples of how the statistic is used in society.
    (2) Make one suggestion that will help this group next time they do a demonstration.

The teacher also gives comments and suggestions to the presenting group.

3. Halfway through the unit, each group completes a checklist on how well the group is using the four co-operative skills. Each group also indentifies one co-operative skill to work on in order to improve their group learning.

Summative Evaluation

1. Students select one completed assignment to hand in to the teacher. The students receive an individual mark from the teacher: a mark out of 10 for accuracy of the student's individual problem-solving approach and a mark out of 5 for revisions based on help from the group. The mark for revisions is designed to reinforce students' awareness of the usefulness of peer assistance.
2. The teacher and students plan for the test at the end of the unit and decide that it should have an individual and a co-operative component. The teacher will design four problem-solving questions to be completed individually and the group will design one problem to solve co-operatively. Students receive an individual mark out of 20 for solutions to the teacher's questions and a group mark out of 5 for the design and co-operative solution to the group question.
3. At the end of the unit, the students individually evaluate their own learning by writing comments on the following questions.
   "Describe something you have learned about problem solving in statistics from working with your group."
   "How has your understanding of the role of statistics in society changed since the beginning of the unit?"

Summary of Marks for the Unit

Test:	50%	Individual	40%
		Group	10%
Homework:	30%	Solutions	20%
		Revisions	10%
Group Participation:	20%		20%

Two Case Studies in Evaluation

The case studies which follow describe how two teachers applied the evaluation practices described in this chapter. There is a detailed narrative in the first case study which describes how the learning process took place throughout the unit. The second case study focuses only on the evaluation activities. Sample evaluation forms are included with each case study.

The evaluation activities presented in the case studies can be applied in every subject area — not just History or Science. In order to illustrate what can be done, the case studies describe four-week units of study with thorough evaluation activities. Evaluation practices need to suit the nature and duration of the learning activity, and the needs of students. For these reasons teachers may want to modify the evaluation practices described in the case studies for their own classroom use.

Case Study in History

This case study begins with a narrative account of a four-week unit. The captions in the inside column highlight the evaluation activities. Following the narrative is an overview plan showing the relationship between the learning objectives of the unit and the evaluation activities. The forms and questions which are used in each of the evaluation activities are included following the overview plan. The case study concludes with a brief description of the grading procedures used by the teacher.

Description of Four-Week Unit

A teacher of secondary-level History is conducting a unit of study on Native Canadian communities. The class is organized in small groups. The groups' projects are part of a year-long focus on research and report writing skills. Each group of four students has selected a Native Canadian community to study.

On the first day, the teacher and students discuss the learning objectives for the project. Together they identify the following objectives which will form the basis for evaluation:

- to develop the research skills of formulating questions, finding sources of information, making point-form notes and classifying the notes by themes;
- to improve the report writing skills of making an outline, writing a report with an opening statement, discussing ideas on a subtopic and concluding in a way which synthesizes information and ideas;
- to understand how the conditions such as geography, work, and family activities affected life in one Native Canadian community;
- to continue developing the skills of working effectively in co-operative groups.

Teacher and students set learning objectives which will form the basis for evaluation. (See Overview Chart, p. 188)

During the first week, the groups brainstorm questions they would like to explore about their chosen communities. They hypothesize and predict answers to their questions. Then, the groups classify their questions into subtopics and determine the information they will need about conditions and events which affect life in the community. The groups designate subtopics for each member to research during the second week. At the end of the second week, the groups talk about the information collected and plan the outline for their written report.

In the third week, each group member writes about a subtopic. At the end of the third week each group integrates the individual accounts into one group report and makes decisions about the introduction, conclusion, headings, and illustrations.

In the fourth week, the groups read each other's reports. In whole class discussion, students ask questions of the other groups and consider similarities and differences in the life patterns among the different communities studied. These discussions help students to synthesize the knowledge they have developed.

Teacher and students plan summative evaluation activities.	At the beginning of the project the teacher and students decide that the teacher will give each student a final mark based on a group mark for the written account, combined with an individual mark for the subsections written by the individual group members.
Teacher and Students develop a project checklist. (See Project Checklist, p. 189)	The teacher and students develop a checklist to help groups plan the steps involved in the project. They decide that academic learning and group interaction will be evaluated throughout the study by the use of progress reports. Once a week the groups reflect on how the work is going. The report sheet asks for information about progress on the academic tasks and tasks the group would like help with. The report sheet also asks the group to identify one co-operative skill it is using well, and one which needs attention in order for the group to carry out its work successfully.
Teacher and students plan formative evaluation activities. (See Weekly Progress Report, p. 190 and Individual Responsibilities Form, p. 192)	
Teacher reviews weekly progress reports and provides assistance.	Each group keeps all progress reports in a folder to which the students can refer when they want to assess their progress or plan the next steps in their work. Throughout the four weeks the teacher visits the groups to examine the folders and to provide support as needed. Reading the students' reflections keeps the teacher informed of the groups' progress and interaction, which she cannot always see.
Groups evaluate their interaction and set goals.	In the first progress report, one group decides that members need to listen more to each other in order to reach agreement on the subtopics to be researched. Another group is unhappy that one person is making the decisions and the group decides members need to try to share the role of leader.
Teacher observes to assess group progress. (See Teacher Observation Form, p. 191)	The teacher circulates to observe each group throughout the four weeks. Towards the end of the first week she observes that several groups are still brainstorming questions. She is concerned that the groups are not ready to identify subtopics for individual research.
Teacher reflects on her observations to understand group needs and plan teaching strategies.	The teacher wonders what form of assistance she should offer. Is a lack of co-operative group interaction interfering with progress? Are the groups not aware of the time frames? Should she assist the groups in developing a work plan and a time schedule?
Teacher seeks students' input to understand their problem.	She decides that sharing her observations with the class and getting student feedback might clarify the problem.
Class discusses the problem.	The class discussion which follows indicates that the groups had not considered a work plan and time frames.
Students develop their own solution. (See Individual Responsibilities Form, p. 192)	The teacher encourages the class to offer suggestions. "We should keep a record of the responsibilities of each group member." "If we take turns checking that everyone is getting work done, we will be sharing the planning."
	With the teacher's guiding questions, the students have proposed their own solution; the class develops an individual responsibilities form to help the groups plan their work.

At the end of the project, the teacher asks the groups to evaluate the group interaction.

As well, students are asked to complete an individual self-evaluation. Reviewing the folders with their weekly progress reports helps the students to carry out their final evaluation.

The teacher responds to the students' individual self-evaluation. The students' insights and the teacher's observations help her to understand what the students learned about working with others. For example, Franco, a shy student, reported on his individual self-evaluation, "I realized by the end of the first week that I wasn't putting in ideas, so others were making the decisions. After that I tried to put more of my ideas in. The others listened and I felt more a part of the group."

The teacher commented in her evaluation of Franco, "I saw the effort you made. You've learned about yourself in this project. Perhaps you could try to achieve the same goals in our class discussions."

Academic learning outcomes are also evaluated by the teacher and by the students.

The groups evaluate their written report.

Students also complete an individual self-evaluation.

The teacher grades the written accounts giving a group mark to reinforce the idea that the group was responsible for the group product. To evaluate the students' individual learning, she grades individuals on the subsections for which they were responsible.

Groups evaluate their interaction. (See "How We Worked Together" Form, p. 193)

Students evaluate their individual learning. (See "What I Learned in this Project" Form, p. 194)

Teacher evaluates group interaction.

Teacher offers support and suggests goals for an individual student.

Students evaluate the group product. (See "Group Evaluation of Our Project" Form, p. 195)

Students individually evaluate their learning. (See "What I Learned in This Project" Form, p. 194)

Teacher evaluates group and individual learning. (See Teacher's Grading Procedure, p. 196)

Comments on the Evaluation Process

While evaluation activities will vary according to the specific needs of teachers and students, the case above illustrates one method for integrating evaluation of the learning process and outcomes. The class discussion of learning objectives and evaluation procedures provided students with objectives to work towards.

Formative evaluation provided information for setting day-to-day goals for learning and teaching. The regular group reflection encouraged students to consider their progress and how group interaction affected their work. The teacher's observation of the groups and the students' regular progress reports informed the teacher of where the groups needed assistance. These activities provided avenues for communication between the teacher and the students.

Summative evaluation provided evidence of learning outcomes. The students' self-evaluations at the end of the project enabled them to reflect on what they had learned. These self-evaluations informed the teacher of the challenges that individual students experienced and the personal goals that some individuals had set for themselves.

Summative evaluation of the academic learning included assessment of the group product and of members' individual contributions to it. Giving a group mark was an appropriate method for assessing the group product. Giving an individual mark enabled the teacher to assess what each student had learned. Each student's final mark was a composite of marks — individual and group. Because the formative evaluation activities informed the teacher of students' learning, the final mark reflected the learning processes as well as the learning outcomes.

Overview Plan and Evaluation Forms

The following overview plan illustrates how the four learning objectives were evaluated during the unit of study on Native Canadian communities. Because research and report writing skills were the primary learning objectives, many of the evaluation activities address these skills. The forms which teacher and students used for each evaluation activity are provided on the following pages.

		Learning Objectives			
		To develop research skills	To improve report writing skills	To understand life in a Native Canadian community	To continue developing co-operative skills
Formative Evaluation	Project Checklist p. 189	▓	▓		
	Weekly Progress Report p. 190	▓	▓		▓
	Teacher Observation Form p. 191	▓	▓	▓	▓
	Individual Responsibilities Form p. 192	▓	▓	▓	▓
Summative Evaluation	The Written Report	▓	▓	▓	
	"How We Worked Together" Form p. 193				▓
	"What I Learned in This Project" Form p. 194	▓	▓	▓	▓
	"Group Evaluation of Our Project" Form p. 195	▓	▓	▓	

Project Checklist

This checklist will help the group to plan the steps involved in the project work. Please check off each task as the group completes it. Add additional steps which your group finds useful.

Planning

- ☐ Did we brainstorm questions to explore the topic?
- ☐ Did we predict possible answers to our questions?
- ☐ Did we sort our list of questions into subtopics?
- ☐ Did we assign subtopics to group members?
- ☐ Did we decide what information we needed?
- ☐ Did we brainstorm possible sources of information?
- ☐ Did we establish time lines for completion?
- ☐ _____

Research

- ☐ Did we plan research time in the school library?
- ☐ Did we help one another by sharing resources?
- ☐ Did we make point-form notes on information we collected?
- ☐ _____

Report Writing

- ☐ Did we plan an outline for the report?
- ☐ Did we discuss ways to display and present our information (text and pictures)?
- ☐ Did we use peer conferences to revise first draft writing?
- ☐ Did we meet to review progress and check time lines?
- ☐ Did we meet to clarify format before second draft writing?
- ☐ Did we read through our group report together?
- ☐ Did we discuss how our report addressed our original questions?
- ☐ _____

Weekly Progress Report

Please use your Project Checklist as a guide in filling out this progress report each week. These reports will help the group to plan weekly work.

What is the current main activity of group members?

_____

_____

_____

_____

What will be the next step?

_____

_____

_____

_____

Is there a task with which you need help? Please describe.

_____

_____

_____

_____

_____

_____

_____

Co-operation in Our Group

One co-operative skill we are using well:

_____

One co-operative skill on which we need to work:

_____

Date _____

Group Members _____   _____

_____   _____

Case Study in History

Teacher Observation Form

Throughout the project, the teacher circulates to observe each group. The teacher notes progress and difficulties. When the teacher observes difficulties, he/she helps the group to find solutions to the difficulties.

Group # _____ Date: _____

Project Work

☐ The group is working on the tasks scheduled for this week (*the teacher may wish to refer to the group's Project Checklist*).

Group Interaction

I see group members:
☐ contributing ideas;
☐ listening to others;
☐ helping others;
☐ synthesizing ideas presented.

A task with which the group may need help is:

_____

_____

_____

_____

A co-operative skill of which this group may need to be aware:

_____

_____

_____

_____

Individual Responsibilities Form

Please use the following headings to keep a record of responsibilities the group assigns to each group member. This chart will help the group and individual members know what each member's responsibilities are. If anyone has difficulty with one of the tasks, consult with the group and seek other members' assistance.

Who	What	When

Case Study in History

"How We Worked Together"

As a group, discuss how well you worked together. Your Weekly Progress Reports may help you in your discussion.

1. Co-operative skills we used that made our work smooth and enjoyable:

_____

_____

_____

2. Co-operative skills we improved during our month's work together:

_____

_____

_____

3. A co-operative skill to work on in the future:

_____

_____

_____

"What I Learned in This Project"

1. Research skills about which I feel more confident:

_____

_____

_____

2. Research skills I would like to improve in the future:

_____

_____

_____

3. A task I helped another group member with:

_____

_____

_____

4. A task someone helped me with:

_____

_____

_____

5. Something I learned about myself as a result of the group project work:

_____

_____

_____

6. Something I learned about another group's topic:

_____

_____

_____

Case Study in History

"Group Evaluation of Our Project"

Now that we have finished discussing the projects in class, discuss and then answer the following questions as a group. The questions will help you to evaluate your strengths and areas for improvement in future project work. Use this scale in the evaluation:

Strongly agree | 1 | 2 | 3 | 4 | 5 | Strongly disagree

1. Our Report Writing Skills

Our report has an opening statement which introduces each of the subtopics.

| 1 | 2 | 3 | 4 | 5 |

Our conclusion answers questions we asked at the beginning of this project.

| 1 | 2 | 3 | 4 | 5 |

Our headings and illustrations (maps, charts, drawings etc.) help the reader understand the report.

| 1 | 2 | 3 | 4 | 5 |

2. Our Research Skills

We made sure that everyone was able to collect enough information on their subtopic.

| 1 | 2 | 3 | 4 | 5 |

Our point form notes were sorted into themes.

| 1 | 2 | 3 | 4 | 5 |

Our outline of main ideas helped us write the first drafts.

| 1 | 2 | 3 | 4 | 5 |

We helped each other revise our first drafts.

| 1 | 2 | 3 | 4 | 5 |

3. Describe two characteristics about the community your group studied which you find interesting. Give reasons why you find them interesting. (*Use the other side of this page as needed.*)

_____

_____

4. Describe any similarities you see between the life circumstances in the community your group studied and in the communities studied by other groups. (*Use the other side of this page as needed.*)

_____

_____

Grading Procedures

The teacher marked the project work in the following manner.

Each group received a mark for the group report out of:	30
Each student received an individual mark for subtopic work out of:	20
Total mark for the unit is:	50

Each student's total mark (out of 50) for the unit is the sum of the group mark for the project report and the individual mark for subtopic work.

Because formative evaluation gave feedback during the month-long work, the mark for the final report reflects the learning process as well as the outcome.

Because the students were encouraged to help each other throughout all phases of the work, a larger portion of marks is assigned to the group than to the individual work.

Because this unit of study takes one month of the four-month term, the students' marks on this project constitute one quarter of the term grade.

Case Study in Science

This case study includes only the evaluation activities. There is an overview plan showing the relationship between the learning objectives of the unit and the evaluation activities. The forms and questions which are used in each of the evaluation activities are included following the overview plan.

A teacher of Intermediate Science conducted a four-week unit of study entitled "Solutions." In small groups, students conducted five laboratory experiments. The teacher wanted to place strong emphasis on procedures involved in experimentation and also on skills required to work productively as a lab crew. Additionally, the teacher wanted to help students incorporate self- and peer evaluation throughout the four-week unit. These became the learning objectives for the unit.

Overview Plan and Evaluation Forms

		Learning Objectives		
		To develop proficiency in carrying out lab experiments	To improve students interactive skills	To help students to identify and apply evaluative criteria
Formative Evaluation	Checklist of Lab Skills (10 marks) p. 198	■		■
	"Thinking about Working Together" Forms (10 marks) p. 199		■	■
	Anecdotal Peer Evaluation of Lab Report p. 200	■		■
Summative Evaluation	Lab Report Submission with Rationale (40 marks) p. 201	■		■
	Co-operative Test (30 marks) p. 202	■		■
	"What Did I Learn" Form (10 marks) p. 203		■	■

Checklist of Lab Skills

Lab groups will be given time after each experiment to complete the checklist below. Please keep all five checklists in your group file folder. At the conclusion of this unit each group will staple the five checklists together in chronological order and hand them in. You will receive a group mark out of 10 for the completeness of your checklists.

There are blank spaces on this checklist so that your group may add activities which it finds helpful in developing proficiency in carrying out lab experiments. Alternatively, your group may need to cross off some of the items on this checklist temporarily in order to focus on specific skills.

		Not at all			*Very thoroughly*	

Preparing

	Not at all				Very thoroughly
Did we discuss the purpose of the experiment?	1	2	3	4	5
Did we predict various possible outcomes?	1	2	3	4	5
Did we read directions carefully?	1	2	3	4	5
Did we organize equipment and materials?	1	2	3	4	5
	1	2	3	4	5

Experimenting

	Not at all				Very thoroughly
Did we use equipment efficiently and accurately?	1	2	3	4	5
Did we observe adequate safety precautions?	1	2	3	4	5
Did we record data systematically?	1	2	3	4	5
Did we follow directions?	1	2	3	4	5
(or adequately design steps to be followed?)					
	1	2	3	4	5

Concluding

	Not at all				Very thoroughly
Did we follow proper clean-up procedures?	1	2	3	4	5
Did we formulate conclusions based on data?	1	2	3	4	5
Did we cite limitations and/or assumptions involved in the experiment?	1	2	3	4	5
	1	2	3	4	5

Lab # _____ Goal for improving lab work:

_____

_____

Signatures: _____ Date:_____

_____

_____

_____

NOTE: This checklist is an example of group self-evaluation. The teacher and students have brainstormed the list of criteria for evaluating lab work at the beginning of the unit. The teacher visits groups throughout the unit and discusses the checklists with each group. Additionally, the teacher may use the checklist as an observation form. The teacher fills it out and then asks the group to compare it with the checklist the group has completed.

"Thinking About Working Together"

You will complete this form twice during the four-week unit. Near the end of the unit the teacher will visit groups to read each member's forms. You will receive an individual mark out of 10 for the completion of the two forms.

The purpose of filling out this form is to help you to consider how you feel and what you think about working in a group. Thinking about the process of working together helps people to recognize strengths and to become aware of ways in which they can improve their working relationships.

Please answer the following three questions on your own. Then use the three questions and your responses as the basis for discussion within your group.

1. How do you feel about your participation as a member of your group at this time?

Please circle:

Very Satisfied   Quite Satisfied   Somewhat Dissatisfied   Quite Dissatisfied

Please comment on why you checked where you did. _____

_____

_____

2. How do you feel about the productivity of your group at this time?

Please circle:

Very Satisfied   Quite Satisfied   Somewhat Dissatisfied   Quite Dissatisfied

Please comment on why you checked where you did. _____

_____

_____

3. What might you, or your group, do to improve group functioning as you continue to work?

_____

_____

_____

Anecdotal Peer Evaluation of Lab Report

After each experiment groups will write up a lab report and file it in the group file folder. After the third experiment each group will exchange its report with another group for anecdotal peer evaluation.

There are three criteria to help your group evaluate the effectiveness of the lab report.

1. **Equal participation**
   Is it clear how each member of the lab crew contributed to the work?
2. **Scientific thought**
   Is there a clear indication that the writers understand the concept being investigated? Do the data support the conclusions?
3. **Clarity**
   Can the report be understood by other readers? Are the diagrams, charts, etc., orderly and relatively simple?

Please write your anecdotal responses in two categories — POSITIVES and CONCERNS. List suggestions for improvement and sign your names to the evaluation report. Use the model below to create a full size form.

Lab Report # _____
Lab Crew:

Criteria	Positives	Concerns
Equal parti-cipation		
Scientific thought		
Clarity		

Suggestions for Improvement:

_____

_____

Names of the Evaluators: Date: _____

_____   _____

NOTE: *The teacher formally models how to write constructive anecdotal peer evaluation by guiding the class through this evaluation form. If students are experienced with peer evaluation the teacher could mark the evaluators by assessing how helpful their anecdotal response is. Alternatively, the teacher could respond anecdotally to the evaluators to provide constructive comments on their evaluation.*

Lab Report Submission with Rationale

You have completed five lab reports. Select one report which your group would like to submit for formal marking. Staple the other four lab reports underneath. Include this one-page rationale as a covering letter.

Your group mark on this assignment will be out of 40 marks.

Rationale for Report Selection (10 marks)
Describe specifically why you selected this report for formal evaluation.

_____

_____

_____

_____

_____

_____

_____

_____

_____

Criteria for Evaluation of Report (30 marks)

5 marks	**Equal participation:** Is it clear how each member of the lab contributed to the work?
20 marks	**Scientific thought:** Is there a clear indication of your understanding of the concept being investigated? Does the data support the conclusions?
5 marks	**Clarity:** Can the report be understood by the teacher and other readers? Are the diagrams, charts, etc., orderly and relatively simple?

NOTE: The three criteria used by the teacher for formal marking of the lab reports have been introduced to the class at the beginning of the unit and are the same criteria which students use to write the anecdotal peer evaluation.

Co-operative Test

Group Members: **Date:** _____

_____

_____

_____

Questions to Evaluate Lab Skills

This test is worth 30% of the final unit mark. Work in your group to answer the first two questions. Use rough paper to write a draft before writing on this paper. Create a third question that your group would like to answer in order to demonstrate your learning. Use the reverse side of this paper to write both the group question and the group answer. (This question and answer will be worth 10 marks.)

(10 marks)
1. Explain one danger of using absolutes like "always" and "never." Use an example from your lab work to illustrate the danger.

_____

_____

_____

_____

(10 marks)
2. Consider the following statement.
   In designing an experiment, usually limits must be put on variables, and only one should be tested at a time.
   Provide an example from your lab work which illustrates this aspect of designing an experiment.

_____

_____

_____

_____

NOTE: After the test has been completed, the teacher may ask each group to report on the question which it created and to explain its answer.

Case Study in Science

"What Did I Learn?"

Name: _____ **Date:** _____

Sit quietly by yourself to reflect personally on the questions on this form. Draft a response and then complete this form. If you are having difficulty getting started you may wish to discuss these three questions with someone else in your group before trying to answer them on your own.

The teacher will collect your form and respond with written comments. The teacher will also give you an individual mark out of 10 for thorough completion of the form. The information on this form will help the teacher to understand what you have learned from working with others over the four week unit.

In what ways does working in your group contribute to your personal development of proficiency in lab work?

_____

_____

_____

_____

What did you learn about yourself from working with others?

_____

_____

_____

_____

In what ways does working in your group help you to evaluate your learning?

_____

_____

_____

_____

Summary

This chapter has described the evaluation process in co-operative small group learning. Formative evaluation of the learning process and summative evaluation of the learning outcomes are essential components. Sensitive anecdotal evaluation by students and teacher contribute to student growth and to the development of classroom programs. Use of a variety of evaluation methods throughout a co-operative learning endeavour will help teacher and students to identify academic and social skills and the positive attitudes which small group interaction encourages.

Criteria for Good Evaluation Practices in Co-operative Small Group Learning: A Summary

Relate evaluation activities to the learning objectives.

- Design evaluation activities which enable students to practise and demonstrate skills needed to achieve the learning objectives.

Evaluate different dimensions of the learning process.

- Practising curriculum skills
- Applying concepts to solve problems
- Organizational and thinking skills
- Co-operative interaction skills
- Students' descriptions of their own learning

Use a variety of kinds of evaluation activities.

- Group progress reports and work plans
- Quizzes, worksheets, assignments
- Observation of groups at work
- Group interaction checklists and reports
- Group discussions
- Projects, presentations, reports
- Tests

Emphasize the helpful, informative purposes of evaluation by involving students in planning, designing, and carrying out evaluation.

- Discuss with students ahead of time:
  - the curriculum themes and learning objectives
  - the kinds of activities to be included in evaluation
  - the criteria for evaluation
- Encourage groups to design evaluation activities for themselves and for others.
- Encourage collaborative quiz-taking:
  - Allow students to work on quiz questions individually then share ideas/answers with peers.
  - Ask groups to discuss the questions to understand what is being asked (for example, terms and key words in questions) before answering individually.
- Provide opportunity for students to learn from their quiz performance by revising and expanding their answers with classmates.
- Provide time for students to share their strengths and to help each other set new learning goals on the basis of quiz outcomes.
- Introduce self-evaluation through anecdotal comments about knowledge, skills and attitudes learned, goals for future learning.

Use formative evaluation for a variety of purposes.

- To identify students' initial interests and ideas about the topic.
- To identify learning progress during a unit of study.
- To identify where the teacher's help is needed.
- To help students set daily learning objectives.
- To determine which parts of the learning activity are working well and which parts need modification.

Use summative evaluation for a variety of purposes.

- To help students reflect on their interests and learning outcomes through participation in evaluation.
- To understand what students have learned by the end of a unit of study.
- To understand how the learning process (academic and group interaction) contributed to the learning outcomes.
- To help students and teacher identify future learning objectives.
- To reflect on the effectiveness of the learning activities.

Resources

One of the purposes of this handbook is to help teachers develop and expand their particular co-operative learning interests. This section includes three kinds of resources: books, articles and newsletters.

The authors of this handbook have used their combined perspectives to shape the understanding of co-operative small group learning described herein. A variety of views is expressed in the sources listed, reflecting the diverse perspectives educators bring to co-operative small group learning.

Books

Aronson, Elliot
The Jigsaw Classroom
Beverly Hills, California: Sage Publications, 1978
An excellent comprehensive explanation of Jigsaw rationale and its application in the classroom.

Barnes, Douglas and Todd, Frankie
Communication and Learning in Small Groups
London: Routledge and Kegan Paul, 1977
An examination of the relationship between language and learning by analyzing transcripts of group learning situations.

Barnes, Douglas
From Communication to Curriculum
Montclair, New Jersey: Boynton/Cook, 1976
Through transcribed conversations from the classroom, Douglas Barnes analyzes the different styles of discourse in use, showing the importance of relatively unstructured conversations in the work of schooling. The author argues that personal and conversational interaction that exists between teacher and student is a crucial aspect of the learning process.

Bossert, Steven
Tasks and Social Relationships in Classrooms
New Rochelle, New York: Cambridge University Press, 1979
A report on the study of the implications of classroom organization for group relations.

Britton, James
Language and Learning
London: Allan Lane, 1976
A comprehensive work providing a sound theoretical rationale for emphasizing the importance of encouraging students to learn through their own language and experience.

Britton, James
Prospect and Retrospect
London: Heinemann, 1982
Selected essays from the works of James Britton covering a span of three decades of theories of language representation and symbolism. Practical implications and applications for classroom work in reading and writing, the value of talk, and the teaching of literature are explored.

Brubacher, Mark, Payne, Ryder, and Rickett, Kemp (Eds.)
Perspectives on Small Group Learning. Theory and Practice
Oakville: Rubicon Publishing, 1990
Essays by top educators provide a synthesis of co-operative and collaborative learning.

Bruner, Jerome
Actual Mind. Possible Worlds
Cambridge, Massachusetts: Harvard University Press, 1986
A collection of essays which explore the part language plays in making experience meaningful. The essay on "Language and Education" is particularly relevant to the small group co-operative learning context.

Clarke, Judy and Wideman, Ron
Co-operative Learning — The Jigsaw Strategy
Scarborough, Ontario: Scarborough Board of Education, Values Education Project, 1985
Order from: Superintendent of Program, Education Centre, Level 2, Scarborough Board of Education, 140 Borough Drive, Scarborough, Ontario, M1P 4N6.
A clear, straightforward description of the use of Jigsaw in the classroom.

Cohen, Elizabeth G.
Designing Groupwork: Strategies for the Heterogeneous Classroom
New York: Teachers College Press, 1984
This book provides an excellent general introduction to co-operative small group learning. Particular emphasis is given to structuring of productive heterogeneous interaction.

Co-operative College of Canada
Co-operation and Community Life
Toronto: Co-operative Resource Centre, 1980
Order from: Co-operative Resource Centre, 252 Bloor Street West, Toronto, Ontario, M5S 1V6.
A manual of activities for children 7 - 14 to help them learn about co-operation, develop co-operative skills, and relate the concept of co-operation to the general community.

Davidson, Neil (ed.)
Co-operative Learning in Mathematics
Don Mills: Addison-Wesley, 1990
Written by experienced mathematics educators, each chapter develops practical ideas for applying co-operative small group learning in mathematics at both the primary and secondary level.

Dias, Patrick X.
Making Sense of Poetry: Patterns in the Process
CCTE Monographs and Special Publications, 1987
Order from: Department of Linguistics, Carleton University, Ottawa, Ontario,
K1S 5B6.
A detailed study which illustrates that students are capable of making sense of poetry on their own, through well-structured small group discussion. A most rewarding way to approach poetry for students and teachers alike.

Dishon, Dee and O'Leary, Pat Wilson
A Guidebook for Cooperative Learning: A Technique for Creating More Effective Schools
Portage, Michigan: Cooperation Unlimited, 1984
Order from: Cooperation Unlimited, P.O. Box 68, Portage, Michigan, 49081.
A clear, step-by-step guide to implementing the Johnsons' model of co-operative learning, this resource stresses basic principles and the teacher's role at each stage.

Glasser, William
Control Theory in the Classroom
New York: Harper and Row, 1986
A compelling rationale for the use of small group co-operative learning presented in a manner that integrates theory and practical application.

Goswami, Dixie and Stillman, Peter
Reclaiming the Classroom: Teacher Research as an Agency for Change
Montclair, New Jersey: Boynton/Cook, 1987
Distributed by Heinemann Educational Books Inc., 70 Court St., Portsmouth, New Hampshire, 03801.
An excellent international collection of articles celebrating teachers as active professionals personally involved in exploring teaching and learning as part of a "community of thinkers" engaged in "action research."

Graham, Neil
Student Evaluation in English
Queen's Park, Toronto: Ontario Ministry of Education, 1987
This resource guide provides practical evaluation suggestions and techniques to help teachers evaluate student success with broader curriculum objectives in English and demonstrates how to integrate student evaluation into the learning process.

Jaques, David
Learning in Groups
New York: Methuen, 1984
A comprehensive account of purposes and techniques of group learning in undergraduate higher education. Written from a British perspective, it is a helpful source of reference and advice on the range of possibilities group work offers teachers.

Johnson, David W. and Johnson, Roger T.
Learning Together and Alone: Cooperation, Competition, and Individualization
Englewood Cliffs, New Jersey: Prentice-Hall, 1975
A stimulating guide for teachers wanting to provide a sensible balance of these three basic goal structures or learning contexts.

Johnson, David W., Johnson, Roger T., Holubec, Edye Johnson, and Roy, Pat
Circles of Learning
Englewood Cliffs, New Jersey: Prentice Hall, 1984
An excellent guide to help educators understand what co-operative learning is, and procedures for implementing and supervising its use.

Joyce, Bruce and Showers, Beverly
Student Achievement Through Staff Development
White Plains, New York: Longman, 1988
A description of a comprehensive system for the support of educational personnel who wish to create more effective schools. Includes a strong rationale for co-operative approaches for both students and educators.

Kagan, Spencer
Cooperative Learning Resources for Teachers
University of California: School of Education, 1985
Order from: Spencer Kagan, School of Education, University of California, Riverside, California, 92521.
A wide-ranging, general manual which contains good new material for implementing Jigsaw, detailed steps for introducing Co-op Co-op, Kagan's streamlined version of Group Investigation, and a synthesis of Jigsaw and Co-op Co-op.

Kreidler, William J.
Creative Conflict Resolution: More Than 200 Activities for Keeping Peace in the Classroom
Glenview, Illinois: Scott Foresman, 1984
Provides a variety of procedures for dealing with conflicts, and includes activities for creating a classroom atmosphere in which conflict is less likely to occur.

Marland, Michael
Language Across the Curriculum
London: Heinemann, 1977
Order from: McLeod Publishing, 30 Lesmill Road, Don Mills, Ontario, M3P 2T6.
A collection of articles that explore the uses of language for learning in every subject area.

Meyer, Carol and Sallee, Tom
Make It Simpler: A Practical Guide to Problem Solving in Mathematics
Reading, Massachusetts: Addison-Wesley, 1983
An excellent, year-long program in problem solving for grades 4-8 which takes about fifteen minutes daily for students working in groups of four.

Moffett, James and Wagner, Betty
Student-Centred Language Arts and Reading, K - 13: A Handbook for Teachers
Burlington, Massachusetts: Houghton Mifflen, 1976
An excellent resource which links theory and practice for all teachers.

Moorman, Chick and Dishon, Dee
Our Classroom: We Can Learn Together
Portage, Michigan: The Institute for Personal Power, 1983
Order from: The Institute for Personal Power, P.O. Box 68, Portage, Michigan, 49081.
Provides practical, teacher-proven ideas for creating a co-operative classroom environment within which team learning methods can be successfully introduced.

Orlick, T.
The Cooperative Sports and Games Book: Challenge Without Competition
New York: Pantheon, 1978
Exciting concepts in play and recreation based on co-operative principles.

Orlick, T.
The Second Cooperative Sports and Games Book
New York: Pantheon, 1982
More exciting concepts in play and recreation based on co-operative principles.

Pepitone, Emmy
Children in Cooperation and Competition
Indianapolis, Indiana: Lexington Books, 1980
Describes differences in the social behaviour of children working at specific tasks and relates these differences to age, sex and socio-economic background.

Reid, Ian
The Making of Literature
Australian Association for the Teaching of Literature, 1984
The primary focus of the book is students responding to literature. Chapter 2, "Learning Through Exchange," examines the role of interactive talk in the reading process.

Reid, Jo-Anne, Forrestal, Peter, and Cook, Jonathan
Small Group Learning in the Classroom
Scarborough, Western Australia: Chalkface Press, 1989
Order from: Chalkface Press, 1 Cobb Street, Box 222, Scarborough, Western Australia 6019, Australia.
A superb description of a variety of classroom organizational strategies for implementing small group learning.

Rhodes, Jacqueline and McCabe, Margaret
Simple Co-operation in the Classroom: Beginner's Guide to Establishing Co-operative Groups
Willits, California: ITA Publications, 1985
Order from: ITA Publications, P.O. Box 1599, Willits, California.
A good text to use as a beginner's guide — describes first steps for teachers who want to use co-operative learning groups.

Salmon, P. and Claire, H.
Classroom Collaboration
London: Routledge and Kegan Paul, 1984
Research shows why students learn better by sharing and exchanging personal experiences related to learning in a student-centred classroom.

Saskatchewan Department of Co-operation and Co-operative Development
Working Together, Learning Together
Saskatoon, Saskatchewan: The Stewart Resources Centre, 1983.
Order from: The Stewart Resources Centre, S.T.F., Box 1108, Saskatoon, Saskatchewan, S7K 3N3.
This eclectic handbook for teachers at any grade level discusses the teacher's roles and provides skills-teaching activities to help create interdependence and interpersonal skills when using co-operative group learning methods.

Schmuck, R. A. and Schmuck, P. A.
Group Processes in the Classroom
Dubuque, Iowa: William C. Brown, 1983
A comprehensive text for educators seriously exploring the whole field of human dynamics in group processes.

Schneidewind, Nancy and Davidson, Ellen
Open Minds to Equity: A Sourcebook of Learning Activities to Promote Race, Sex, Class and Age Equity
Old Tappan, New Jersey: Prentice Hall, 1983
A year-long curriculum of lesson plans and activities to help students become aware of and confront inequity issues, and to develop skills in working together.

Sharan, Shlomo, Hare, Paul, Webb, Clark D., and Hertz-Lazarowitz, Rachel (eds.)
Cooperation in Education
Provo, Utah: Brigham Young University Press, 1980
Order from: Brigham Young University Press, Business, 205 UPB, Provo, Utah, 84602.
Based on proceedings of the first International Conference on Cooperation in Education, Tel-Aviv, Israel, July 1979, the first four chapters provide useful teacher manuals for implementing Group Investigation (Sharan), Jigsaw (Aronson), Student Team Learning (Slavin) and an introduction to the use of small group methods in teaching mathematics.

Slavin, Robert E.
Cooperative Learning
New York: Longman, 1983
A summary of hundreds of studies demonstrating the effectiveness of non-competitive learning.

Slavin, R., Sharan, S., Kagan, S., Hertz-Lazarowitz, R., Webb, C., and Schmuck, R. (eds.)
Learning to Cooperate, Cooperating to Learn
New York: Plenum Press, 1985
A collection of articles based on the proceedings of the Second International Conference on Co-operation in Education, Provo, Utah, July 1982. Many excellent contributions including "Creating a Co-operative Learning Environment: An Ecological Approach" by Nancy and Theodore Graves.

Torbe, Mike and Protherough, Robert
Classroom Encounter
London: Ward Lock, 1976
A collection of articles on the relationship between language and learning including transcripts of student discussions.

Torbe, Mike and Medway, Peter
The Climate For Learning
London: Ward Lock, 1981
An exploration of contexts in which learning can take place in the classroom. This book offers a psycholinguistic rationale for learning through peer interaction.

Vacha, Edward, Mcdonald, William, Coburn, Joan, and Black, Harold
Improving Classroom Social Climate: Teacher's Handbook
New York: Holt, Rinehart and Winston, 1979
This handbook provides a variety of classroom activities for grades 4-6 for dealing with issues of attraction, communication, leadership, norms, expectations, and classroom cohesion.

Wells, Gordon
Learning Through Interaction
Cambridge University Press, 1981
Based on the Bristol Study of Language Development, this book argues that conversation provides the central context of language development. The child learns through exploring his/her world in interaction with other people.

Articles

Brubacher, Mark and Payne, Ryder. "The Team Approach to Small Group Learning." *Indirections* 10 (March 1985): 9-19.

Clarke, Judy and Wideman, Ron. "A Piece of the Puzzle." *Forum* 12 (September/October 1986): 38-41.

Cavanagh, Gray and Styles, Ken. "Small Group Projects: an Improved Model." *Indirections* 8 (December 1983): 64-76.

ERIC Clearinghouse on Urban Education. "Cooperative Learning in the Urban Classroom." *Equity and Choice* (Winter 1987): 15-18.

Featherstone, Helen (ed.). "Cooperative Learning." *Education Letter* Harvard Graduate School of Education. II (September 1986): 4-6.

Gilbert-MacMillan, Kathleen, and Leitz, Steven J. "Cooperative Small Groups: A Method for Teaching Problem Solving." *Arithmetic Teacher* (March 1986): 9-21.

Gough, Pauline B. "The Key to Improving Schools: An Overview with William Glasser." *Phi Delta Kappan* 68 (1987): 656-662.

Johnson, David W. and Johnson, Roger T. "Cooperative Small-Group Learning." *NAASP Curriculum Review* 14 (October 1984).

Joyce, Bruce, Showers, Beverly, and Rolheiser-Bennett, Carol. "Staff Development and Student Learning: A Synthesis of Research on Models of Teaching." *Educational Leadership* 45 (October 1987): 11-23.

Kagan, Spencer. "Cooperative Learning and Sociocultural Factors in Schooling." In *Beyond Language: Social and Cultural Factors in Schooling Language Minority Students.* Los Angeles, California: Evaluation Dissemination and Assessment Center, California State University, 1986.

Lennon, Gail. "Co-operative Learning: No One Can Learn Alone." *The FWTAO Newsletter* (February/March 1988): 1-7.

Madden, Nancy A. and Slavin, Robert E. "Effects of Cooperative Learning on the Social Acceptance of Mainstreamed Academically Handicapped Students." *The Journal of Special Education* 17 (1983): 171-182.

Medway, Peter and Goodson, Ivor. "The Feeling is Mutual: Possibilities of Cooperative Learning between Students and Teachers." *Times Educational Supplement* 31, 34 (June, 1975): 17.

Myers, John. "Co-operative Learning Techniques and Mainstreaming; a Toronto Example Joining Teachers and Students." *Newsletter, Council for Exceptional Children, Ontario Provincial Federation* 24 (October, 1986): 1,3.

Myers, John and Taylor, Marnie. "Cooperative Techniques in the Classroom." *Multiculturalism* 3 (1983): 7-10.

Nickolai-Mays, Susanne, and Goetsch, Kristine. "Cooperative Learning in the Middle School." *Middle School Journal* (November 1986): 28-29.

Owen, Heleen. "Cooperative Classrooms: Implementing Cooperative Learning. One District's Experience." *Equity and Choice* (Winter 1987): 19-26.

Parker, Ruth, E. "Small-Group Cooperative Learning - Improving Academic, Social Gains in the Classroom." *NASSP Bulletin* (March 1985): 48-57.

Rasinski, Timothy, and Nathenson-Mejia, Sally. "Learning to Read, Learning Community: Considerations of the Social Contexts for Literacy Instruction." *The Reading Teacher* (December 1987): 261-264.

Rasinski, Timothy V. "Caring and Cooperation in the Reading Curriculum." *The Reading Teacher* (March 1988): 632-634.

Schniedewind, Nancy and Solend, Spencer J. "Cooperative Learning Works." *Teaching Exceptional Children* (Winter 1987): 22-25.

Slavin, Robert E. "Developmental and Motivational Perspectives on Cooperative Learning: A Reconciliation." *Child Development* 58 (October 1987): 1161-1167.

Slavin, Robert E. "Small Group Instruction." In *The International Encyclopedia of Education, Research and Studies* Vol. 8, New York: Pergamon Press, 1985.

Smith, Roy A. "A Teacher's Views on Cooperative Learning." *Phi Delta Kappan* 68 (May 1987): 663-666.

Stallings, June A. and Stipek, Deborah. "Research on Early Childhood and Elementary School Teaching Programs." M.C. Wittrock (ed.) *Handbook of Research on Teaching, Third Edition.* New York: MacMillan Publishing Co., 1986. See especially pp. 746 ff.

Uttero, Debbra A. "Activating Comprehension Through Cooperative Learning." *The Reading Teacher* (January 1988): 390-394.

Yeomans, Anne. "Research Report: Collaborative Group Work in Primary and Secondary Schools: Britain and the USA." *Durham and Newcastle Research Review X* (Autumn 1983): 99-105.

Ziegler, Suzanne. "Cooperative Learning." *SCOPE* (publication of Research Services, Toronto Board of Education, January 1987).

Newsletters and Magazines

Co-operative Classroom
The Great Lakes Association for the Study for Co-operation in Education, available from Sue Ferguson, Area East Office, Toronto Board of Education, 885 Dundas St. East, Toronto, Ont. M4M 1R4

The Co-op Forum
Newsletter of the Co-operative Resources Centre at The Ontario Institute for Studies in Education, available at 252 Bloor St. West, Room 12-110, Toronto, Ont. M5S 1V6

I.A.S.C.E. Magazine
International Association for Studies in Co-operative Education, available from Nancy and Ted Graves, 136 Liberty Street, Santa Cruz, California, 95060

The Co-operative Link
Co-operative Learning Centre, available from: 202 Pattee Hall, University of Minnesota, Minneapolis, Minnesota, 55455

Student Team Learning Newsletter
Johns Hopkins Team Learning Project, available from the Centre for Social Organization of Schools, 3505 N. Charles Street, Baltimore, Maryland, 21218

Video

Together We Learn

This video program is designed to explore initial questions teachers have regarding co-operative small group learning and to stimulate discussion. The following questions may help to focus further discussion on issues related to implementation:

- What current objectives/concerns of our students could co-operative learning address?

- What teaching practices are necessary to carry out co-operative learning?

- What topics would we like to explore in more detail (evaluation, forming groups, kinds of groups, etc.)?

- What are ways we could get started?

- How could teachers in our school help each other in carrying out co-operative learning?

The video program complements this handbook and is available from: The Metropolitan Toronto School Board, Educational Resources Department, 45 York Mills Road, Willowdale, Ontario, M2P 1B6. Telephone: (416) 489-3332.

Index to Evaluation Forms